Hannah Arendt ⌖ Aung San Suu Kyi

Charlotte Brontë ⌖

Cather ⌖ Colette ⌖

Dickinson ⌖ Annie Dillard ⌖ H.D.

Isabelle Eberhardt ⌖ George Eliot ⌖

ls through Ruth White) ⌖ Joan Halifax

Lessing ⌖ Anne Morrow Lindbergh

Gabriela Mistral ⌖ Marlo Morgan ⌖

⌖ Katherine Anne Porter ⌖ Ayn Rand.

Olive Schreiner ⌖ Mary Shelley ⌖

tinghoff ⌖ Alice Walker ⌖ Simone Weil

n Post Wolcott ⌖ Mary Wollstonecraft

Wright ⌖ Marguerite Yourcenar ⌖

The
Words of a Woman

The
Words of a Woman

Christine Mary McGinley

CROWN PUBLISHERS, INC.
NEW YORK

Published by Crown Publishers, 201 East 50th Street, New York, New York 10022. Member of the Crown Publishing Group.

Random House, Inc. New York, Toronto, London, Sydney, Auckland

www.randomhouse.com

CROWN is a trademark and the C & SUN Design is a registered trademark of Random House, Inc.
Design by Lauren Dong

Printed in the United States of America

Library of Congress Cataloging-in-Publication Data
McGinley, Christine Mary.
The words of a woman / Christine Mary McGinley.—1st ed.
    I. Women—Drama. I. Title
    PS3563.C36398W67   1999   98-52332
                                    CIP

ISBN 0-609-60411-2

10 9 8 7 6 5 4 3 2 1
First Edition

for the spirits

For making all the difference,

Brenda Sodt Foster, Connie Dunlap, Robert Klaus,
Sybill Navas, Jim Ford, Frank Potter,
my mother, and my family

DeAnna Heindel,
Georges Borchardt, Inc., Literary Agency, New York

Ann Patty,
Crown Publishers, Inc., New York

I thank you from my heart.

Special thanks

Annette DePetris, Joel Goldberg, Bill O'Donnell
Diane Lloyd, Ruth Wagman, Wiete Liebner
Marty Smith, Jim Pompe, Ron Austin
Mary Ann Andersen, Andrea Spreter, Andra Pekelsma
DePaul University School for New Learning
Vail Friends of the Dance and Vail Valley Theater Company
Reina Schratter, Carlton Rochelle,
New York University Fales Library
University of Michigan Library
Chicago Cultural Center
Ann Arbor Public Library
Carol Lasser, Oberlin College
New York Public Library
Marin County Public Library
National Public Radio

CONTENTS

PREFACE

*I*t is with tremendous debt to its many authors that *The Words of a Woman* exists as a creative work as well as a tribute to the great women whose voices it has joined together. Composed entirely of excerpts from the written works of more than fifty extraordinary women, the piece is a literary mosaic, perhaps a literary stained-glass window, where each splendid fragment sparkles anew in the light that shines through the final mosaic.

The fragments making up this mosaic, though removed from their original contexts and intricately intertwined, retain the style of their authors as much as possible; words have been italicized and punctuation added for dramatic emphasis only. The actual literary jewels from which *The Words of a Woman* is composed are displayed following the text.

The process of selecting, editing, and interlacing such finely crafted prose and poetry was understandably haunted throughout by a sense of sacrilege. At the same time, there has been an abiding certainty that every one of the women whose words are included in *The Words of a Woman* would be proud to be associated with all the other women and take some pleasure in the final piece.

Although this mosaic does cast a beam of light on some remarkable females, many of whom have been neglected by mainstream education, this was its privilege, not its purpose. Like all creative works, this one took on a life of its own. *The Words of a Woman* does not begin to include all great female writers, nor does it represent the finest of those whose words have given form to this piece. Instead, it would hope to inspire further exploration of the wealth of wisdom and pure enjoyment found in great literature.

INTRODUCTION

*T*he inspiration for *The Words of a Woman* came from Virginia Woolf. In her wonderful book about women and writing, *A Room of One's Own*, she asks us to imagine that Shakespeare had a sister who was brilliantly gifted, as Shakespeare was, but who never wrote a word. She did not write, or even read, because it was not acceptable in her day for a female to learn to read or write; young women were expected to learn to darn socks and cook the stew. Her extraordinary gifts—as extraordinary as her brother's—were never put to use.

"Now my belief is that this poet who never wrote a word and was buried at the crossroads still lives. She lives in you and in me, and in many other women . . . for great poets do not die; they are continuing presences; they need only the opportunity to walk among us in the flesh . . . For my belief is that . . . if we have the freedom and the courage to write exactly what we think . . . then the dead poet who is Shakespeare's sister will put on the body which she has so often laid down. Drawing her life from the lives of the unknown who were her forerunners, as her brother did before her, she will be born."

I discovered *A Room of One's Own* at precisely the time in my life when I needed to read it. I had always wanted to devote myself entirely to my own creative work. In that moment, when I was seized by the spirit of Shakespeare's sister, I was overcome by a deep sense of commitment and an exultant sense of urgency. I did not imagine how thoroughly I would be consumed—I spent the next six years completely immersed in great literature by women.

What Virginia Woolf aroused in me, George Sand blasted through my being. Her direct voice in *Histoire de ma vie* and *Lettres d'un voyageur* breathed life and form into an ethereal female spirit. I saw a woman alone on a stage; she stood completely exposed and absolutely forthright. She represented all the female artists and thinkers and writers who had gone before her—all the Shakespeares who would have been, had they not been sisters. She spoke on behalf of all the women who would now step forward to claim their birthright—their own voice of creative expression.

"This is not a part I am playing, it is not a duty, it is not even calculated; it is an instinct and a need . . . Write your own history, all of you who have understood your life and sounded your heart. To that end alone I am writing my own."

After reading George Sand's letters and memoirs, Virginia Woolf's *A Writer's Diary*, Doris Lessing's *A Small Personal Voice*, and *The Journal of Katherine Mansfield*, I became particularly drawn to works that contained the most self-disclosure. I read novels and poetry and short stories, but then sought out the private personal reflections of the artist, the insight *into* the artist, often buried within otherwise pedestrian letters or hidden amongst the diary's depictions of uneventful days. My exploration of female literature became a treasure hunt. The more I read, the more jewels I discovered and the more I was compelled to read.

With each new artist came new reflections of my own feelings, my own search, my struggle to create, to write. Was I indeed the carrier of something that had propelled George Sand and Virginia Woolf and Jane Austen and Katherine Mansfield and Olive Schreiner and all the other women whose words I was now devouring? They all felt the same thing inside; I was convinced of it. They were all driven to write, yes, but there was another distinct current of energy that ran through each of them and that struck a resonant chord in me—we were *women*.

But female writers are not any different from male writers, are they? A writer is a writer is the contemporary view. Just as a corporate executive is a corporate executive, a senator is a senator. Or in our eagerness to equate "equal to" with "same as," are we missing some very significant differences? If a writer is simply a writer, why would it be ludicrous to think of a project that highlights great literature by men? Why when scouting for great literature by women was I invariably directed to "feminist" work? Is the feminist perspective what distinguishes femaleness in literature? Has the feminist dynamic itself diminished the distinguishing features of *femaleness?* My personal search for the heart and psyche of women writers became more meaningful as it evolved.

My own list of great women of literature grew: Jane Austen and Emily Dickinson and the Brontës were joined by Katherine Mansfield and Sarah Orne Jewett and Eudora Welty and Willa Cather and Edith Wharton and Flannery O'Connor and Annie Dillard. Mary Shelley held me entranced. I saw in Elizabeth

Barrett the soul to which Robert Browning surrendered his heart. The density of George Eliot stretched both my reach and grasp. Gertrude Stein defied me to discover what inspires her following, and the challenge made the moment of discovery particularly sweet. Alice Walker's razor's edge grew smooth and fluid as her poetry penetrated. Doris Lessing spoke about education in words everyone on the planet should hear, and Marguerite Yourcenar laid bare every human being's responsibility for our environment and our world. Ting Ling moved me as though she had bled through her pen. She and Anna Akhmatova and Gabriela Mistral made the global human experience so immediate, so present.

Each writer led me to other writers. I also asked teachers and scholars and artists and friends to share with me their favorites, to help me discover the new or uncover the obscure, to reach outside my experience and exposure as a white middle-class American. (Because of Toni Morrison's *Playing in the Dark,* I will never again be unaware of my own "literary whiteness.") Of all the people involved in the process, I am most indebted to my French friend Nelly Vaïsse who introduced me to Marguerite Yourcenar, a woman so full of wisdom and the gift of articulation that I am both proud and humbled to acknowledge the bulk of *The Words of a Woman* that belongs to her. Yourcenar lighted my way to an obscure French writer, Jeanne de Vietinghoff, and it would have been worth the years of searching just to know this one woman through the words she wrote.

At one point I realized my discoveries were not exclusively from great literature; I was exploring in a larger realm of extraordinary women. Florence Nightingale and Marie Curie and Mother Teresa had left indelible marks in history; their written words were important and powerful. The philosophy of Simone Weil shook me to the core. Isadora Duncan spoke of life and art as only the great dancer Isadora could. The tortured soul of Isabelle Eberhardt, a tragic nineteenth-century North African wanderer, cried out to me through her memoirs which were found in the wreckage of her disastrous circumstances. And Aung San Suu Kyi—one of the most courageous human-rights activists—her words belonged in this piece. As did the spiritual insights of naturalist Machaelle Small Wright and Buddhist-anthropologist Joan Halifax, and the wonderful message Marlo Morgan carried back to the U.S. from the Aborigines.

What was my allegiance to great literature? What was I discovering here in the words of great women? And where was I going with this project? The answer was clear. I would continue to read all the exceptional women I discovered and let the writings themselves guide the process. The focus would be entirely on the words. At this point I knew that some final work would be entitled simply *The Words of a Woman.*

Within a few years I had assembled an immense collection of literary gems, excerpts I had pulled from hundreds of writings by the remarkable women I had come to know. Throughout endless hours in the company of these female spirits, I found myself communicating with them, even aloud, laughing with them, celebrating new discoveries, compelling connections between their words; they seemed to gravitate toward one another. It was as though a composite persona had emerged from the pages and was guiding the flow of editing and weaving, molding the piece to her expression, to convey her message. I found myself in one of the most fluid and exhilarating processes I have ever known, when neither the course nor the objective was completely clear. What I knew with certainty was that the product of this incredible process would possess a value all its own.

The building of a mosaic is an appropriate description of this process. From each of these women I have gained another piece of a larger understanding of life, of humanness, of *femaleness.* One of the most pronounced insights has been of how profoundly penetrating the eye of a woman can be, how powerful her influence can be, when she is simply *being*—not carrying a banner for women or fighting for the rights of women, but being one. The voice I have heard in the words of these women is one that is often lost in the confusion of our changing roles, in our efforts to find an equality at the same time that we hold on to the precious differences that can make a perfect wholeness of the male-female dynamic. The voice I have come to recognize as *the female voice* is not a voice *for* women or *about* women. It is not even a voice unique to women. It is the female voice that exists in all of us—a voice some say we as a society are just beginning to hear, and that we would do well to listen to it.

What does one do with a literary mosaic with a female voice? The original image of a woman on a stage remained with me. Could a theatrical work actually be composed of such an extraordinary collection of literary excerpts? The final piece included the words of more than fifty women of diverse life experiences from around the globe and through centuries of time, excerpts from great novels and poetry and prose, from diaries and letters, essays and interviews and speeches. Could the very real and very singular woman who had emerged and guided me through this process actually be heard by an audience? Could this mosaic of melded energies possibly affect anyone else the way it was affecting me?

Emerson says that genius is believing that what is true for us in our own private heart is true for all humanity. But no matter how deeply we believe in something, until it actually resonates with other human beings, there is a sense of incompleteness about it. Until that moment, when we are assured we are not alone, even truth is not quite enough. It is this response that I believe every artist seeks; it is for this response that we create.

On December 9, 1995, I presented *The Words of a Woman*, a literary mosaic and one-woman play, at the Ann Arbor Civic Theater. The literary company I had been keeping for the past few years had pushed me head-long into a brand-new dimension of personal exposure. I could hardly believe I was sitting on a stage in front of an audience, an obsessed writer masquerading as an actress. The excruciating anxiety about this utterly untried creation was something I survived only by being accompanied by some of the most formidable females of all time. And their truth was my truth:

"You finally do have to give something terribly intimate and secret of yourself to the world and not care, because you have to believe that what you have to say is important enough . . . to give yourself away and take the consequences, whatever they are." And the words of May Sarton were echoed by Jeanne de Vietinghoff: "To give yourself for what you are, and seek to be worth much, in order that you may give much."

I was also fortified by the vivid memory of some extraordinary theatrical experiences—Julie Harris' portrayal of Emily Dickinson, Judith French's Jane Austen, Irene Worth's Edith Wharton, Eileen Atkins' superb Virginia Woolf. I had learned from these actresses that great literature delivered honestly can indeed reach people. The power of their performances relied entirely on the strength of the character who wrote the words and on the command of the words themselves, no contrived movement, just a sincere delivery accompanied by the natural physical responses the words evoke. This was an incredible challenge.

During that eternity on the stage in Ann Arbor, one could have heard a needle drop in the theater. The silence terrified me. Afterward, as I stood alone in the dark backstage, I did not know how I would ever console myself for the abysmal failure of my coming-out as an artist. I told myself that I could at least feel gratified that I had put myself out there and survived it. The audience had applauded so I knew they would be polite at the reception; I just had to get through it. As I walked the dark hallway to my fate, I was greeted by a black man who was coming backstage to see me. I looked into his face and saw tears in his eyes. He said, "Thank you. I can't tell you how much I needed to hear that." I could see that he had been deeply moved. Standing with that man for that moment holding his hands and looking into his face, I remembered a promise I had made to myself: If my work had been worthwhile for one person, I would consider it a success. I will never forget that man or that moment.

To my surprise and inexpressible joy, that man was not alone in his response. I learned that the silence in the theater was the silence of people listening intently to every word. I have since been invited to several venues around the country, where each time the performance has been received with the same reverent stillness. People were listening to the *words.* And even more thrilling was their eagerness to read the piece, to be with it again, to examine the "seamlessness" and the illusion of one voice, to ruminate on the passages that had swept them away.

The tremendous power of the relationship between author and reader was affirmed again in the unmistakable passion of the audience members who spoke to me. Their eyes would lock with mine as they recited the passage that had struck them like a thunderbolt; they could not wait to know the identity of the author and the work. I knew that as soon as they could get to a library or a bookstore they would be exploring their new discovery and relishing every word. Each time, as I took such pleasure in speaking of the author, I shared again in that wonderful relationship—the connection we feel with someone we know intimately, someone we have come to know only through their writing.

Although my presence onstage could not begin to do it justice, *The Words of a Woman* had indeed taken form. From the moment of its conception, that moment with Shakespeare's sister, it was destined to be brought to life. It was destined to be experienced through the profound intimacy that is uniquely theater. But this little piece of theater took its form from great literature. And great literature must be read. It must be absorbed and handled and contemplated and cherished, and be available to be revisited again and again.

All my life I had struggled to find my own voice as an artist. I could feel it reverberating inside of me. Why could I not give form to it? How could my most essential self be so elusive? I believe even artists spend much of their lives thinking of the creative process as something that is willed into being. The very arrogance of being human has fooled us into believing that all things begin with our intelligence. We have so surrounded ourselves with things that are the products of our conceiving and planning and working, we forget that we ourselves are but tiny specks in a much larger process. I know now that the creative process is something that happens to us. It finds us and fuses with us and takes up residence, and makes it impossible for us to give to it anything less than all of the energy it deserves.

Six years ago, when I became deeply and obsessively immersed in great literature by women, I knew only that my soul needed to do this. I had no idea that in the process I would be finding my own voice. I have learned that the appreciation of greatness is as important in our lives as the ability to achieve it. These women have taught me to aspire not to greatness but to honesty, that not everything which is honest will be great, but nothing which is dishonest can be.

Through *A Room of One's Own* and indeed her entire body of work, Virginia Woolf has been a galvanizing force in the emergence of great women writers. I believe she would be the first to remind us that great writing is never created to balance the scales for women, not even for the centuries of women who were denied self-expression. To write anything worthwhile, she asserts, we must write for ourselves. Although the spirit of Shakespeare's sister "lives in you and in me and in many other women," I was not compelled to create *The Words of a Woman* for Shakespeare's sister, nor for all the luminous female spirits with whom I have had the great pleasure of colliding. This was a thoroughly selfish exercise, which has nourished me in ways I cannot begin to enumerate. Above all, it has taught me to believe in my own spirit, to remain unflinchingly faithful to it, and to keep writing.

PROLOGUE

*I*magine that we are hidden observers in a woman's private writing room. The time we will spend with her is just a glimpse of the endless hours she spends alone at her writing desk and with her books, intimately involved with words.

She possesses the animation of a person for whom words are living creatures, for whom thoughts and ideas offer rich companionship. Though her words are those of a deep contemplative, her boundless energy and her playfulness come through in the exaggerated roll of a phrase, the sudden eruption of another, in her physical participation in her verbal expression. Her thoughts and feelings flow; some burst forth, others unfold before her as she speaks. The connections between her thoughts may be apparent in her words or they may reveal themselves through her response to the words.

The stage is set simply with a single pool of light illuminating a writing desk and chair placed on an antique rug. A favorite lamp, familiar books, a framed photo, a treasured paperweight, tulips in a crystal vase—all make the desk her own.

She enters, deeply immersed in reading, her diary in one hand, a cup of tea in the other. She begins reading aloud, as though trying to absorb the words:

"Just as appearing beings living in a world of appearances have an urge to show themselves, so thinking beings which still belong to the world of appearances"—she stops and looks off into the distance and then inserts a new thought—"even after they have mentally withdrawn from it"—then returns to reading aloud—"have an urge to speak, and thus to make manifest what otherwise would not be a part of the appearing world at all."

The words evoke a curious thoughtfulness, which prompts her to sit on the top of the desk, settle in, turn to the first page, and read aloud, "Where shall I begin?" She looks out into the darkness of the theater. She casually closes the book and places it on the desk next to her. As she continues to speak, it becomes apparent to us that we are hearing the words she is writing in her diary.

The Words of a Woman

here shall I begin? Never was a work—if indeed this can be called a work—less planned, devoid of heroes and plots. Were it not that writing has a definite appeal, sometimes intoxicating, which makes us forget the unknown witness and be carried away by our subject, I don't think we would ever have the courage to write about ourselves—unless we had a great deal of good to say. No one will fail to agree that such was not my case, and that it required a great deal of daring, or a great deal of thoughtlessness, to talk about myself.

What sort of diary should I like mine to be? Something loose knit and so elastic that it will embrace anything that comes into my mind. I should like it to resemble some deep old desk into which one flings a mass of odds and ends without looking them through. To come back, after a year or two, and find the collection had sorted itself, and refined itself, and coalesced, into a work of art. The main requisite, I think, is to put aside everything that is merely an envelope, an appearance—and go directly to the heart. To write as the mood comes, and of anything whatever, since I am curious to find how I went for things put in haphazard, and to find the significance to lie where I never saw it at the time.

The adolescent I used to be, and even the child I remember having been, somehow did sense something of what my life and work would turn out to be. What I recall is not so much the comradeship of other children as something inside me that was *awake* to every *detail,* a power with which I was in deep communion whenever I was alone with nature. I was a healthy girl—loved running and swimming and romping—yet no children of my own age, and none even among the nearest of my grown-ups, were as close to me as the great voices that spoke to me from books.

I was always of a determined, and if thwarted, violent disposition—an almost proud consciousness. I am grateful for this excessive frame of mind. Aiming at tranquillity, I have almost destroyed all the energy of my spirit, almost rooted out what renders it estimable.

My temper *was* sometimes violent, my passions vehement, but by some law in my temperature they were turned toward an eager desire to *learn,* and not to learn all things indiscriminately. I confess that neither the structure of languages, nor the code of governments, nor the politics of the various states possessed attractions for me. It was the secrets of heaven and earth that I desired to learn, the substance of things, the inner spirit of nature, the mysterious soul. I am one of those adolescents who have never forgotten their first encounter with Plato.

I love life with greater *urgency* than most. There is a love for the marvelous, a *belief* in the marvelous which hurries me—a quality that was with me from the beginning and has never since been still. My mind will be suddenly flooded by that quality and feeling a human sometimes has, being on top of the world and not exactly part of it anymore—those luminous waves that overpower one with joy in the rich, throbbing complexity of life.

I have a faithful joy and a joy that is lost—something profound and terrible—in this eternal desire to establish *contact.* Why is there not a *discovery* in life?! Something one can lay *hands on* and say, *"This is it!"* I have an astonishing sense of something *there,* which is *it.* It is not exactly beauty that I mean. It is that the thing is in *itself* enough. A sense of my own strangeness is there too, of the infinite oddity of the human position. I used to feel this as a child—couldn't step across a puddle, I remember, for thinking, How strange, what am I? Who am I? What is the truth of human life? These questions are always floating about in me. And then I bump against some exact fact—a person, a book—and come to a great sense of freshness. I think I do fairly frequently come upon this *it.*

We are all of us constantly undergoing initiation. Every accident, every incident, every experience of joy or suffering is an initiation. Even the words that I'm speaking at this very moment are working a change in me. Learning *stamps* you with its moments. Childhood's learning is made up of moments. It isn't steady. It's a pulse.

In a children's art class, we sat in a ring on kindergarten chairs and drew three daffodils that had just been picked out of the yard; and while I was drawing, my sharpened yellow pencil and the cup of the yellow daffodils gave off whiffs just alike. That the pencil doing the drawing should give off the same smell as the flower it drew seemed part of the art lesson— as shouldn't it be? A child sees everything, looks straight at it, examines it. Most people, after they are about eleven or twelve, quite lose this power, they see everything through a few preconceived ideas—the dogmas of party, country, class, religion—all of them uncompromising.

Did you ever do what I was very fond of doing when I was a child? I used to call it "looking at things really." Look at your hand, for instance; make an effort of mind, and dissociate from it every preconceived idea. Look at it simply as an object which strikes the eye. You will be surprised how new and strange and funny it looks, as though you had never seen it before. It can be done with the other senses. Listen to people talking just as a mere noise striking the ear.

Children use all their senses to discover the world. Then artists come along and discover it the same way, all over again. Or now and then we'll hear from an artist who's never lost it.

In my sensory education I include my physical awareness of the word. Of a certain word, that is; the connection it has with what it stands for. At around age six, perhaps, I was standing by myself in our front yard waiting for supper, just at that hour in a late-summer day when the sun is already below the horizon and the risen full moon stops being chalky and begins to take on light. There comes the moment, and I saw it then, when the moon goes from flat to round. For the first time it met my eyes as a globe. The word *moon* came into my mouth as though fed to me out of a silver spoon. It had the roundness of a Concord grape Grandpa took off his vine and gave me to suck out of its skin and swallow whole in Ohio.

There are days when my life seems to have been a golden legend studded with precious jewels; when my mind is like a stained-glass window through which I see marvelous forms and richest colors; when an idea seems a ray of genius, or when I actually believe my art is a resurrection. Just as there are other days when I look through dull gray glass; when the past seems but a series of catastrophes, the future a certain calamity—my art, the hallucinations emanating from the brain of a lunatic.

I believe most people are aware of periods in their lives when they seem to be "in grace" and other periods when they feel "out of grace"—they may use different words. In the first happy condition, one carries all one's tasks before one lightly as if borne along on a great tide; in the opposite state, one can hardly tie a shoestring. A large part of life consists in learning a technique of tying the shoestring, whether one is in grace or not. But there are techniques of living, too; there are even techniques in the search for grace. I have learned, by some experience, and by the writings of countless others before me, also occupied in the search, that certain environments, certain modes of living are more conducive to inner harmony than others. Simplification of life is one of them.

To have a home and a family and a definite means of livelihood, to be a useful cog in the social machine, all these things seem necessary, even to those who think of themselves as wholly liberated. And yet such things are only a *different* form of slavery. For those who have the courage to obey the voice in their hearts, there remains a home even were they in the desert.

Life tends to shackle us, to stifle in us the real being that we are, and which it is our *duty* to emancipate and expand! Once we are securely fettered—by family ties, by the obligations of our career—all individual growth is checked, and we become the plaything of circumstance. We connect happiness with outward advantages rather than inner realities; it is more difficult to surrender ourselves to the inner gods of whose presence none save ourselves are conscious, than to adapt our souls to the conventional forms of happiness. But we depend less on what happens in our lives than on what *passes* in our souls!

He who understands this no longer lives in the satisfaction of a duty accomplished, or in the hope of a realized dream, but in the immortal richness of his intimate experiences. It is an absorbing interest which he carries with him everywhere he goes, and which is renewed and enriched at every contact with life.

Now, the writer, as I think, has the chance to live more than other people in the presence of this reality. It is his business to find it and collect it and communicate it to the rest of us. The hand which holds the pen and the body and soul which are attached to it are things of infinitesimal importance for those who love the truth. After all, if a thing is true, it must come to thousands of minds, it must live in millions of hearts, and that is what makes the use of a writer—not that he expresses what no one else thinks and feels, but that he is the voice of what others feel.

I personally prize the stimulators most; I like a book you can only read a few pages of and then you have to throw it down, you have so many thoughts of your own. I have never fully analyzed what this stimulating power is. Art is as incomprehensible in its ultimate essence as light or time or space. And it is always a search for something for which there is no market demand—something new and untried, where the values are intrinsic and have nothing to do with standardized values. We become creators when, after the innumerable stages of adaptation to external influences, we finally grasp what is really our own, what we *receive* as a personal message.

Certain writing friends whose judgment I admire have told me my writing lacks detail, exact observation of the physical world, my characters hardly ever have features, or not enough—that they live in empty houses, et cetera. At one time, I was so impressed by this criticism, I used to sit before a landscape and note literally every object—every color, stick, and stone before my eyes. But when I remembered that landscape, it was quite simply not in those terms that I remembered it, and it was no good pretending I did, and no good attempting to describe it, because it got in the way of what I was really trying to tell.

Writing, in any sense that matters, cannot be taught; it can only be learned, and learned by each one of us in his own way. You have to give something terribly intimate and secret of yourself to the world and not care, because you have to believe that what you have to say is important enough. To give yourself for what you are. And seek to be worth much, in order that you may give much. And whether it matters for ages or only for hours, nobody can say. But to sacrifice a hair of the head of your vision, a shade of its color, in deference to someone with a measuring rod up his sleeve, is the most abject treachery—the greatest of human disasters a mere *fleabite* in comparison!

It is all very well to say we should *disregard opinions.* Unfortunately, it is *precisely* the nature of artists to mind excessively what is said of them. Literature is strewn with the wreckage of those who have minded beyond reason the opinions of others.

I wonder if in heaven our *best* thoughts—*poets'* thoughts, especially—will not be flowers somehow, or some sort of beautiful live things that stand about and grow and don't have to be bought and sold. Selling our writing seems as bad as selling our fellow beings.

Someone asked me whether it was difficult or easy to write poetry. I answered that when somebody dictates it to you, it's easy, but that when there is nobody dictating—it's *quite* impossible.

To be a poet is to have a soul so quick to discern, so quick to feel, that no shade of quality escapes it—a soul in which knowledge passes instantaneously into feeling, and feeling flashes back as a new organ of knowledge. One may have that condition by *fits* only.

At its best, the sensation of writing is that of any unmerited grace. You search, you break your heart, your back, your brain, and then, and only then—it is *handed* to you. Nobody whispers it in your ear. It is like something you memorized once and forgot. Now it comes back and rips your breath away. You lay it down cautiously, and then you wait, suspended—rearing and peering from the bent tip of a grassblade—until the next one finds you.

How many moments have I lost—if I can call them lost—with flowers. It is a pleasure sweet to a writer to witness the rebirth of a tulip in a crystal goblet. The ink dries on the pen while before me a creation raises itself to perfection, and *will* attain it, shine for a day, perish the next.

> *Letting go*
> *in order to hold on*
> *I gradually understand*
> *how poems are made.*

The leftover love.
The love that spills out
of the too full cup
and runs and hides
its too full self
in shame.

I gradually comprehend
how poems are made.
To the upbeat flight of memories.
The flagged beats of the running
heart.

It would be a thousand pities if women wrote like men, or lived like men, or looked like men, for two sexes are *quite* inadequate, considering the vastness and variety of the world, how ever should we manage with only one?!

Male and *female* are in fact perpetually passing into one another. There is no wholly masculine man, no purely feminine woman. The true feminine is beyond the whole question of subjection and domination and inequality. It is the catalytic power which is essential to all creativity. As long as humanity continues to evolve, to separate ourselves from the chaos, to express ourselves in a higher form, we must create. With the active involvement in restoring the true feminine energy there lies great hope. We should all be among those who, with Rodin, *bow* before the toilsome effort of the thinker, and who, with Pasteur, "never doubt that knowledge and peace will triumph over ignorance and war."

There should, I think, be basic courses at a very simple level, which would teach children that they are living in the midst of the universe on a planet whose resources they will need to conserve, that they depend on the air and the water and on all living creatures. They would learn that men have killed one another in wars that have never done anything but lead to other wars, and that every country doctors its history to make itself look good. They would learn enough about the past to feel a bond to the men and women who have gone before them. They would know the names of plants and be taught about animals. (It's a major step forward to realize that the form we happen to be accustomed to living in is not the only one in which life dwells; life can come with wings instead of arms, with eyes more acute than ours, with the intelligence of the dolphin, our equal in brainpower, though its image of the world is surely different from ours.) They should learn how to give first aid to the injured. Teachers would also instill the simple ethical ideas without which life in society is impossible. In religion, no practice or dogma would be imposed, but something would be said about all of the world's great religions—to kindle respect for religion in the child's mind and eliminate hateful prejudices. (What one believes matters little; what matters is *how* one believes.) And children should be taught to love work, provided it is useful, that no human pursuit achieves dignity until it can be called work, and that the worth of a human creature will always be proportionate to the strength of his effort. Above all, teachers should teach children that the only thing that really matters in life is the human beings with whom one is thrown into contact, the souls one touches; that of all the offspring of earth and heaven, love is the most precious. What I am proposing would be, for the first time in history, a humane education.

In the meantime it would be a help at least to call things by their right names, for every child, repeatedly, throughout his or her school life: "You are in the process of being indoctrinated. What you are being taught here is an amalgam of current prejudice and the choices of this particular culture, molded to fit into the narrow and particular needs of this particular society. We are sorry, but it is the best we can do. We have not yet evolved a system of education that is not a system of indoctrination. By the time you reach the age when you have to choose (we still take it for granted that a choice is inevitable) between the arts and the sciences, you may choose the arts because you feel here is humanity! freedom! You do not know that the choice itself is the result of a false dichotomy rooted in the heart of our culture. Those of you who are more robust and individual will find ways of educating yourself—educating your own judgment. *Not* by measuring your knowledge, but by admitting the grandeur of the unknowable, will you attain the greatest measure of justice in your life. And remember, for all the words we have in print, there are as many that have never reached print, have never been written down. History, even social ethic, are taught by means of stories. The real history of Africa, for instance, is still in the custody of black storytellers and wise men—black historians. It is a verbal history, still kept safe from the white man and his predations. Everywhere, if you keep your mind open, you will find the truth in words not written down. So never let the printed page be your master. And learn to follow your own intuitive feeling about what you need."

Just as appearing beings living in a world of appearances have an urge to show themselves, so thinking beings, which still belong to the world of appearances, even after they have mentally withdrawn from it, have an urge to speak, and thus to make manifest what otherwise would not be part of the appearing world at all.

It is not that in my pride I want to suggest that I am isolated by my opinions because of my exceptional greatness or intelligence. No. I am a creature riddled with faults and weaknesses, and the thickest veils of ignorance shroud my mind's brightest insights. I am *alone* as a result of disenchantment and shattered illusions; who has not also seen his own turn to dust? But there was one I had in particular, vast and beautiful, such as my soul was in those early years. That one proved to be the seal of everlasting calamity. But all this would require a great deal more space and a kind of history of my youth.

The companions of our youth always possess a certain power over our minds which hardly any later friend can obtain. They know our infantine dispositions, which however they may be afterward modified, are never eradicated.

> *No matter how far away you are, you still remain—*
> *Like a presence that will never fade,*
> *Like the landscape of my life.*

What a bad joke the human heart is! I feel at times I understand love; in the end I can never really explain it—the sweetest and yet the bitterest thing we know. So *remarkably* educational, it would be a great pity to miss it. For real love, like all truly mystical things, is one of the bridges to the spirit;

opens the doors to *everything* as far as *I* can see, including and perhaps most of all, one's own secret and often frightening real self.

If someone were to ask my advice about spending their life so much alone as I have, I would have to say you do feel the knocks. There is nothing to stand between you and the world; the blows come straight on the bone. But when I am working, when I am *absolutely in it,* I believe I am the happiest person in the world. I wish the gods would give me three hundred years to *live* and to *write.* Only when one is connected to one's own core can one be truly connected to others. For me, the core, the inner spring, is best found through solitude.

One thing is beautiful to me, I have not lost one grain of my faith in love. I know I shall never create better than when I do so for the love of some human creature, and under the influence of that divine feeling. For no art, no ambition, no joy can replace the marvelous unfolding which true love brings to the soul. For so many people, love seems to be simply a fortuitous circumstance. For others, it is life itself.

No one but a genius should think of writing on misty, voluptuous nights! An all-powerful desire dominates the senses, perturbs the heart, *shakes* the heart without warning, like a whirlwind swoops on an oak.

What IS the mystery of *passion,* this electricity we speak of, whose changes make us well or ill, whose lack or excess blasts, whose even balance revives? What is this *influence* that plays over our nerves like fingers on a stringed instrument, and calls forth now a sweet note, and now a wail—now an exultant swell? It seems to come on without our exactly knowing *why,* without our *at all* knowing why for *this* person rather than for *that,* and to go

THE WORDS OF A WOMAN

off again after a while, as it came, also without our knowing *why*. Is there a good and a bad angel who take it in turns to breathe upon this miserable organ, this heart we talk about so much? This *diaphragm*, which expands in response to a cup of coffee! If it is nothing but a blood-soaked sponge, where do these sudden aspirations, these tremors come from? How can anguish suddenly burst from it when certain syllables reach our ears, or from some uncanny resemblance? What is it that makes some of us in the middle of dinner parties—noise and merriment—begin to *sob* without knowing why?

It is truly a suffering which has no name, no clear purpose—a suffering without truce and without end—which one endures, *not* because of the evil one has been guilty of, but through the virtue one has made one's own. The belief in *happiness*. For those who have from childhood believed in the possibility of realizing their inner ideals, the craving for happiness is an instinct as ineradicable as it is necessary. The deadly shock arising from the encounter of the highest conceptions with brutal realities is the supreme injustice. But the more our feeble hope is flung and broken against the deceptions of life, the more surely will it rise, even as the flower can only unfold through the withering of its sheath.

Just as the ugly caterpillar is the beginning of the splendid butterfly, our vision, our strength and our courage come from our own spirit—that other vast reality, lying at the core of every heart, though few will admit it—we know it more intimately than anything else. It is the force in the depths of our soul that in all our victories or defeats ceases not to urge us *forward*.

It is, after all, of small importance if our inferior self is victor or vanquished in this strange crisis we call life. Our only real transgression is that unseen and infinitely subtle act—it happens in the secret place of our being—a wrong we do, not to others, but to ourselves. We are guilty of it every time we disobey what we have recognized as being the best and the *highest* in us. Our deepest instinct, named in turn—intuition, inspiration, grace—remains the most real, and possibly the only immortal part of us. It abides when all else is gone. It promises us the continuance of that which we are, and the plenitude of that which we shall *one day be*. It is the instrument of progress and the truth of the future—that truth which must prevail— that the spirit of humanity can transcend the flaws of our own nature.

It is because of this tendency to use my brain as a magnifying glass that I have always found reality *lacking* in grandeur. It has taken time to accept it, and to find in it specific beauties and things to admire, other than those I sought. Not by dreaming about life can we learn to know it! But by *living* it. And it is through our collision with reality that we prove our grain. I still love to adorn reality, however beautiful it may be. Such a tendency denotes neither the artist nor the poet, I know; it denotes the madman!

> *Much Madness is divinest Sense—*
> *To a discerning Eye—*
> *Much Sense—the starkest Madness—*
> *'Tis the Majority*
> *In this, as All, prevail—*
> *Assent—and you are sane—*
> *Demur—you're straightway dangerous*
> *And handled with a Chain—*

As it happens, the issues that concern and upset me have as yet captured the interest of only a minority of my compatriots, but I believe these issues will become increasingly important as time goes by. The destruction of the planet, the extinction of whole species which is tipping the vital equilibrium between ourselves and our environment, the confrontation of each of us with ourselves and with God—however that word be interpreted. (I have some long and tall thoughts on the subject of God's working through nature, but I will not inflict them on you now.)

We in the "developed" world have many auditory strategies that insulate us from our deeper identity. We have filled our world with noises—mindless tunes, the crackling of "news"; the television set holds young and old in a time trance! The sound of suffering in the world is covered over by the ceaseless song of longing for more—things and more things. We fill our homes and our offices, and the overflow finds its way into crowded storage lockers. Time in our culture is scheduled to the minute. We believe in what we see immediately ahead of us. And when we begin to sense the fabricated nature of who we are, we put on another hat, find another job, change religions or relationships. *Oblivion* is a stupid monster that is devouring generations.

We need to relearn how to *look* at things as they are! If we lift ourselves and *soar high,* we can see a view where a much bigger picture is taking place. We see a vast universal truth which is present *everywhere* within the life force of nature. We see that we do not have a separate self, a self that does not include sun and wind, earth and water, creatures and plants and one another. All of life everywhere, it is all one. Our ancestors, our children, all humanity and all of life course through our veins. And if their ceaseless flow happens to have chosen the path of a particular society and family, the one in which one happens to have grown up, that is just one accident among the many that shape one's life. Our true *identity* is about *relationship* and *process.* Every relation, every gradation of nature is *incalculably* precious. Each of us has more power over the world than we imagine. To *contradict evidence.* To *affirm the unknowable.* To *will the impossible.* Two or three people! with the right sort of *receiving brains* could turn the whole tide of human thought, could bring the whole force of truth and consciousness back into the world!

What we may do, each of us, is to exert a tiny influence, whether it be waking one impulse of love in another soul, or painting a picture, or discovering a beautiful sequence in the nature of the universe and sharing it with others—to leave behind us a world a little more beautiful than it was, even if that world extends no farther than our backyard or kitchen.

I shall never *be* a scientist, making vast discoveries, nor a great leader, nor a mother, devoting myself entirely to the joy of rearing my children. I shall never find out if I have the power for music or painting I have always felt I have. In my little handful of life I shall know few things; but *this* I have—a full, adult, living, breathing *life.* I want to enter *into* it, to *learn* from it, to lose all that is superficial and acquired in me and to become a conscious, direct human being. I want, by understanding myself, to understand others. I want to be *all* that I am capable of becoming. And I *want* to be *writing.* I must speak by such means as are within my reach.

I've had a wonderful new idea for a wild story. The conscious transmigration of a soul. Awakening, the soul seeks to substantiate its true essence and finds itself faced with two possibilities—the resignation of its ideal, or the risk of being crushed by remaining faithful to it. It has surrendered itself to its own power through all the joyous and disturbing fluctuations of existence. It is pure because it has suffered. It waits patiently until it acquires all the force necessary to break its bonds and forge a passage toward a larger future, a fuller destiny. The new spirit demands more than the established order, more than unconscious contentment. It vibrates with a certainty that each soul is fitted for a joy entirely individual. But it must *dare* in order to succeed: dare to *see*, dare to *believe*, and with a childlike purity of heart, dare to be happy. "This is the new duty! To give oneself as one is. To let life meet us as it really is. To *live* in the moment, and extract from *each* moment all that it holds. To have faith in one's own heart. And to not impose a direction on destiny, but to let ourselves be led where fate will lead us. For life is everywhere. True life. With all its heroic struggles and sublime moments."

As I looked at it this morning, it began well and may end well, but there is a long way to go. I don't want to force it; I want to watch and see how the idea unfolds. I want to trace my own process.

And what is to become of all these diaries? I daresay there is a little book in them, if the scraps and scratchings were straightened out a bit. God knows.

I did have a moment of quiet panic at how much of me has been given away. But I decided one does not lose one's soul for giving it away. To gain that which is worth having, it may be necessary to lose everything else.

I really only ask for *time.* Time to write my books. To work with my *hands* and my *feeling* and my *brain.* And if my books are read, if my words reach one person, a single one, and help that person in some way, if only for an instant, then I will consider my life a useful one.

Write your own history!, *all of you* who have understood your life and sounded your heart. To that end alone I am writing my own.

[Lights fade.]

The
Authors' Words

Where shall I begin? I have so many matters to tell you of, that I cannot wait any longer before I begin to put them down.

JANE AUSTEN: *Letters to her sister*

Never was a work—if indeed this can be called a work—less planned . . . were it not that writing has a definite appeal—often painful, sometimes intoxicating, but ever irresistible—which makes us forget the unknown witness and be carried away by our subject, I don't think we would ever have the courage to write about ourselves—unless we had a great deal of good to say. However, reading these letters no one will fail to agree that such was not my case, and that it required a great deal of daring, or a great deal of thoughtlessness to talk about myself for two whole volumes.

I mention all this so that those of my readers who are addicted to novels and accustomed to see me do nothing worse may forgive me for my misguided decision to come on-stage myself in the place of rather more sedate characters who possess all the required trappings to appear in public. As I have said, it was at those times when my tired brain was devoid of heroes and plots that, like an impresario whose company is late for the performance, I came forward worried, distraught and not dressed for the part, to speak as best I could the prologue to the awaited play. But I do believe, on the other hand that certain intimate letters, certain apparently insignificant events in an artist's life, may present, for those who are interested in the secret workings of the human heart, the best introduction to his works and their clearest exposition.

GEORGE SAND: *Lettres d'un voyageur*

What sort of diary should I like mine to be? Something loose knit and yet not slovenly, so elastic that it will embrace anything, solemn, slight or beautiful that comes into my mind. I should like it to resemble some deep old desk, or capacious hold-all, into which one flings a mass of odds and ends without looking them through. I should like to come back, after a year or two, and find that the collection had sorted itself and refined itself and coalesced, as such deposits so mysteriously do, into a mould, transparent enough to reflect the light of our life, and yet steady, tranquil compounds with the aloofness of a work of art. The main requisite, I think on reading my old volumes, is . . .

VIRGINIA WOOLF: *A Writer's Diary*

I should like to put aside everything that is merely an envelope, an appearance, a surface, in order to go directly to the heart of this rose, to the bottom of this sweet chalice.

MARGUERITE YOURCENAR: *That Mighty Sculptor, Time*

. . . not to play the part of censor, but to write as the mood comes or of anything whatever; since I was curious to find how

I went for things put in haphazard, and found the significance to lie where I never saw it at the time.

VIRGINIA WOOLF: *A Writer's Diary*

The adolescent I used to be, and even the child I remember having been, somehow did sense, obscurely and with the utmost confusion, something of what my life and work would turn out to be. But innumerable circumstances and countless events hide the broad outline of a life from view. Perhaps these 'mysterious operations' will become clearer when . . . the day's warm fog gives way to dusk's sharp outlines. Apparently I haven't quite reached that point.

MARGUERITE YOURCENAR: *With Open Eyes*

What I recall of those rambles is not so much the comradeship of the other children, or the wise and friendly talk of our guide, as my secret sensitiveness to the landscape—something in me quite incommunicable to others, that was tremblingly and inarticulately awake to every detail of wind-warped fern and wide-eyed briar rose, yet more profoundly alive to a unifying magic beneath the diversities of the visible scene—a power with which I was in deep and solitary communion whenever I was alone with nature.

EDITH WHARTON: *A Backward Glance*

I was a healthy little girl who loved riding, swimming and romping; yet no children of my own age, and none even among the nearest of my grown-ups, were as close to me as the great voices that spoke to me from books.

EDITH WHARTON: *A Backward Glance*

I was always of a determined, and if thwarted, violent disposition . . . My mind is naturally independent and spurns that subserviency of opinion which is generally considered necessary to feminine softness. But this is a subject on which I must always feel strongly for I feel within me an almost proud consciousness of independence which prompts me to defend my opinions and yield them only to conviction!

ELIZABETH BARRETT BROWNING:
Glimpses Into My Own Life and Literary Character

I am grateful to my earliest years for having given me this excessive frame of mind. When I was crossed, I would be shaken with fury: where did these rages come from? I have not explained it satisfactorily in my memoirs and I cannot do any better now. But I still think they were good for me. I set off on the right foot. To be sure, that in itself is not enough.

SIMONE DE BEAUVOIR: *All Said and Done*

I have examined myself lately with more care than formerly, and find that to deaden is not to calm the mind. Aiming at tranquillity, I have almost destroyed all the energy of my soul— almost rooted out what renders it estimable.

MARY WOLLSTONECRAFT: *Memoirs*

My temper was sometimes violent, and my passions vehement; but by some law in my temperature they were turned not toward childish pursuits but to an eager desire to learn, and not to learn all things indiscriminately. I confess that neither the structure of languages, nor the code of governments, nor the politics of various states possessed attractions for me. It was the secrets of heaven and earth that I desired to learn; and whether it was the outward substance of things or the inner spirit of nature and the mysterious soul of man that occupied me, still my enquiries were directed to the metaphysical, or in its highest sense, the physical secrets of the world.

MARY SHELLEY: *Frankenstein*

I am one of those adolescents who have never forgotten their first encounter with Plato.

MARGUERITE YOURCENAR: *With Open Eyes*

God arranges all sorts of pain for us before we die to make us patient and to prevent us from rushing toward death too eagerly. Me? My time is brief, so I love life with greater urgency than most.

TING LING: *I Myself Am a Woman*

There is something at work in my soul which I do not understand. I am practically industrious—painstaking, a workman to execute with perseverance and labour—but besides this, there is a love for the marvelous, a belief in the marvelous, intertwined in all my projects, which hurries me out of the common pathways of men, even to the wild sea and unvisited regions I am about to explore.

MARY SHELLEY: *Frankenstein*

My sanguine nature encouraged this exactingness, a quality that was with me from the beginning and that has never left me since. I have always insisted on carrying my desires, refusals, acts and thoughts right through to the end. One does not insist unless one reckons on obtaining what one calls for, both from others and from oneself: and there is no getting it unless one does call for it.

SIMONE DE BEAUVOIR: *All Said and Done*

It was the same tremor that had stirred in me in the spring woods of Mamaroneck, when I heard the whisper of the arbutus and the starry choir of the dogwood; and it has never since been still.

EDITH WHARTON: *A Backward Glance*

It's amusing to see how, even on my microscopic field, minute events are perpetually taking place illustrative of the broadest facts of human nature . . . I was thinking of something that interested me very much and my mind was suddenly flooded by one of those luminous waves that sweep out of consciousness all but the living sense and overpower one with joy in the rich, throbbing complexity of life . . .

The Journal of Alice James

. . . worked very early in the morning, and very late a couple of evenings too, trying to get the wierd, strange quality and feeling that a human sometimes has in seeing mountains and being 'on top of the world,' and not exactly a part of it any more.

MARION POST WOLCOTT: letters

> *I have a faithful joy*
> *and a joy that is lost.*
> *One is like a rose,*
> *the other, a thorn.*

The one that was stolen
I have not lost.
I have a faithful joy
and a joy that is lost.
I am as rich with purple
as with sorrow.
Ay! How loved is the rose,
how loving the thorn!
Paired as twin fruit,
I have a faithful joy
and a joy that is lost.

GABRIELA MISTRAL: *Richness*

There is something profound and terrible in this eternal desire to establish contact.

The Journal of Katherine Mansfield

I have some restless searcher in me. Why is there not a discovery in life? Something one can lay hands on and say 'This is it!' . . . I'm looking: but that's not it—that's not it. What is it? And shall I die before I find it? . . . I have a great and astonishing sense of something there, which is 'it.' It is not exactly beauty that I mean. It is that the thing is in itself enough: satisfactory; achieved. A sense of my own strangeness, walking on the earth is there too: of the infinite oddity of the human position . . .

VIRGINIA WOOLF: *A Writer's Diary*

Life is, soberly and accurately, the oddest affair; has in it the essence of reality. I used to feel this as a child—couldn't step

across a puddle once, I remember, for thinking how strange—
what am I . . .

VIRGINIA WOOLF: *A Writer's Diary*

What is the truth of human life, and who can find it? God
Himself would be puzzled. In the midst of all this anguish and
delight; this filth and this luminous purity; this fleshly body
filled with hell fire, and this same body alight with heroism and
beauty—where is the truth? God knows, or the devil knows—
but I suspect they are both puzzled.

ISADORA DUNCAN: *My Life*

Who am I, what am I, and so on: these questions are always
floating about in me: and then I bump against some exact fact—
a letter, a person, and come to them again with a great sense of
freshness. And so it goes on. But on this showing, which is true,
I think, I do fairly frequently come upon this 'it'; and then feel
quite at rest.

VIRGINIA WOOLF: *A Writer's Diary*

We are all of us constantly undergoing initiation. Every accident, every incident, every experience of joy or suffering is an
initiation.

MARGUERITE YOURCENAR: *With Open Eyes*

I do not believe in an irrevocable, foreordained destiny: we
change our destinies constantly as we make our way through
life. Everything that we do affects our fate for better or for
worse. The circumstances into which we are born also exert a

tremendous influence; we come into the world with debits and credits for which we are not responsible already posted to our account; this teaches us humility. But everything is constantly changing inside us as well as outside. Even the words that I'm speaking at this very moment are working a change in me.

MARGUERITE YOURCENAR: *With Open Eyes*

Learning stamps you with its moments. Childhood's learning is made up of moments. It isn't steady. It's a pulse. In a children's art class, we sat in a ring on kindergarten chairs and drew three daffodils that had just been picked out of the yard; and while I was drawing, my sharpened yellow pencil and the cup of the yellow daffodils gave off whiffs just alike. That the pencil doing the drawing should give off the same smell as the flower it drew seemed part of the art lesson—as shouldn't it be?

EUDORA WELTY: *One Writer's Beginnings*

A child sees everything, looks straight at it, examines it, without any preconceived idea; most people, after they are about eleven or twelve, quite lose this power, they see everything through a few preconceived ideas which hang like a veil between them and the outer world.

The Letters of Olive Schreiner

People need to relearn how to love the human condition as it is, to accept its limitations and its dangers, to take a hard look at things as they are, and to renounce the dogmas of party, country, class, and religion—all of them uncompromising and hence doomed.

MARGUERITE YOURCENAR: *With Open Eyes*

. . . did you ever do what I was very fond of doing when I was a child (I used to call it looking at things really) look at your hand for instance, make an effort of mind, and dissociate from it every preconceived idea. Look at it simply as an object which strikes the eye. You will be surprised how new and strange and funny it looks as though you had never seen it before. (I used to do it often in Church to pass away the time.) It can be done with the other senses. Listen to people talking just as a mere noise striking the ear. It is utterly different from what one fancies.

The Letters of Olive Schreiner

Children, like animals, use all their senses to discover the world. Then artists come along and discover it the same way, all over again. Here and there, it's the same world. Or now and then we'll hear from an artist who's never lost it. In my sensory education I include my physical awareness of the word. Of a certain word, that is; the connection it has with what it stands for. At around age six, perhaps, I was standing by myself in our front yard waiting for supper, just at that hour in a late summer day when the sun is already below the horizon and the risen full moon in the visible sky stops being chalky and begins to take on light. There comes the moment, and I saw it then, when the moon goes from flat to round. For the first time it met my eyes as a globe. The word "moon" came into my mouth as though fed to me out of a silver spoon. Held in my mouth the moon became a word. It had the roundness of a Concord grape Grandpa took off his vine and gave me to suck out of its skin and swallow whole, in Ohio.

EUDORA WELTY: *One Writer's Beginnings*

Just as there are days when my life seems to have been a Golden Legend studded with precious jewels, a flowery field with multitudes of blossoms, a radiant morn with love and happiness crowning every hour; when I have found no words to express my ecstasy and joy of life; when the idea of my School seems a ray of genius, or when I actually believe that, although not tangible, my School is a great success; when my Art is a resurrection; so there are other days when, trying to recollect my life, I am filled only with a great disgust and a feeling of utter emptiness. The past seems but a series of catastrophes and the future a certain calamity, and my School the hallucination emanating from the brain of a lunatic . . . So, on some imaginative days, my mind is like a stained-glass window through which I see fantastic beauties—marvelous forms and richest colours, and, on other days, I look only through dull, grey-glass windows and view the dull grey rubbish heap called Life.

ISADORA DUNCAN: *My Life*

I believe most people are aware of periods in their lives when they seem to be 'in grace' and other periods when they feel 'out of grace,' even though they may use different words to describe these states. In the first happy condition, one seems to carry all one's tasks before one lightly, as if borne along on a great tide; and in the opposite state one can hardly tie a shoe-string. It is true that a large part of life consists in learning a technique of tying the shoe-string, whether one is in grace or not. But there are techniques of living too; there are even techniques in the search for grace. And techniques can be cultivated. I have learned by some experience, by many examples, and by the writings of countless others before me, also occupied in the search, that certain environments, certain modes of life, certain rules of conduct are more conducive to inner and outer harmony than others. There are, in fact, certain roads that one may follow. Simplification of life is one of them.

ANNE MORROW LINDBERGH: *Gift from the Sea*

To have a home, a family, a property or a public function, to have a definite means of livelihood and to be a useful cog in the social machine, all these things seem necessary, even indispensable, to the vast majority of men, including intellectuals, and including even those who think of themselves as wholly liberated. And yet such things are only a different form of slavery.

ISABELLE EBERHARDT: *The Oblivion Seekers*

The healthy wayfarer sitting beside the road scanning the horizon open before him, is he not the absolute master of the earth, the waters, and even the sky? His empire is an intangible one, for his domination and enjoyment of the whole vast earth, are things of the spirit.

ISABELLE EBERHARDT: *The Oblivion Seekers*

For those who have the courage to sacrifice their happiness, their rest, their ideal and their religion in order to obey the voice of God in their hearts, there remains a home even were they in the desert; for they have felt that at the bottom of this void something lives, something more real than their firmest faith—their pious hopes, more intimate than the secret of their thoughts, the beating of their hearts; something more marvelous than the rapture of their young happiness; something so vast that it embraces all their aspirations, so high that no happenings can reach it . . .

JEANNE DE VIETINGHOFF: *The Understanding of Good*

Life tends to shackle us, to stifle in us, perhaps by family ties, by the obligations of our career, or by social and religious influences, the real being that we are, and which it is our duty to emancipate and expand. Once securely fettered we are lost; all individual growth is checked and we become the plaything of circumstances.

JEANNE DE VIETINGHOFF: *The Understanding of Good*

We have accustomed ourselves to connect our idea of happiness with outward advantages rather than with inner realities, and we are inclined to doubt the justice of that fate which holds spiritual beauty as its only reward.

JEANNE DE VIETINGHOFF: *The Understanding of Good*

It is more difficult to surrender ourselves to the inner gods of whose presence none save ourselves are conscious, than to adapt our souls to the conventional forms of happiness.

JEANNE DE VIETINGHOFF: *The Understanding of Good*

I possess all, wherever I may be, if I am able to feel all; for we depend less on what happens in our life than on what passes in our soul.

JEANNE DE VIETINGHOFF: *The Understanding of Good*

He who understands these things no longer lives in the satisfaction of a duty accomplished or in the uncertain hope of a realized dream, but in the immortal richness of his intimate experiences. The unfolding of his true humanity, in which he takes part as at the unrolling of a miraculous scene, brings him intense emotions; it is an absorbing interest which he carries with him everywhere he goes and which is renewed and enriched at every contact with life.

JEANNE DE VIETINGHOFF: *The Understanding of Good*

What is meant by 'reality'? It would seem to be something very erratic, very undependable—now to be found in a dusty road, now in a scrap of newspaper in the street, now in a daffodil in the sun. It lights up a group in a room and stamps some casual saying. It overwhelms one walking home beneath the stars and makes the silent world more real than the world of speech—and there it is again in an omnibus in the uproar of Piccadilly. Sometimes, too, it seems to dwell in shapes too far away for us to discern what their nature is. But whatever it touches, it fixes and makes permanent. That is what remains over when the skin of the day has been cast into the hedge; that is what is left of past time and of our loves and hates. Now the writer, as I think, has the chance to live more than other people in the presence of this reality. It is his business to find it and collect it and communicate it to the rest of us.

VIRGINIA WOOLF: *A Room of One's Own*

In the operation of writing, the hand which holds the pen, and the body and soul which are attached to it, with all their social environment, are things of infinitesimal importance for those who love the truth. They are infinitely small in the order of nothingness.

SIMONE WEIL: *Gravity and Grace*

After all, if a thing be true, it must come to thousands of minds, it must live in millions of hearts; and that makes the use of a writer: not that he expresses what no one else thinks or feels, but that he is the voice of what others feel.

The Letters of Olive Schreiner

I personally prize the stimulators most; I like a book you can only read a few pages of and then you have to throw it down you have so many thoughts of your own. I have never fully analyzed what this stimulating power is, but it is possible only to a very complex nature, and it is the result of seeing things with something of that wonderful real complexity that exists in life.

The Letters of Olive Schreiner

As vast and incomprehensible in its ultimate nature as light or time, or space, or matter generally, is that other vast reality, which we know and feel more intimately than anything else in the universe, the will within us that is not time nor space, that is not light nor heat; incomprehensible in its ultimate essence by our puny intellects as is everything else in the universe, yet never for a moment to be ignored . . .

The Letters of Olive Schreiner

Writing ought either to be the manufacture of stories for which there is a market demand—a business as safe and commendable as making soap or breakfast foods—or it should be an art, which is always a search for something for which there is no market demand, something new and untried, where the values are intrinsic and have nothing to do with standardized values.

WILLA CATHER: *On the Art of Fiction*

Man is born to create; in creating he becomes himself, accomplishes his destiny. His whole life is only an initiation into the creative power. To create is not merely to produce a work; it is to give out one's own individuality. Man becomes a creator when, after the innumerable stages of adaptation to alien influence, he finally grasps what is really his own, what he receives, not from men, but directly from God as a special personal message.

JEANNE DE VIETINGHOFF: *The Understanding of Good*

Certain writing friends whose judgments I admire, have told me I lack detail, exact observation of the physical world, my people hardly ever have features, or not enough—that they live in empty houses, et cetera. At one time, I was so impressed by this criticism, I used to sit on a camp stool before a landscape and note down literally every object, every color, form, stick and stone before my eyes. But when I remembered that landscape, it was quite simply not in those terms that I remembered it, and it was no good pretending I did, and no good attempting to describe it because it got in the way of what I was really trying to tell.

*The Collected Essays and Occasional Writings of
Katherine Anne Porter: On Writing*

Writing, in any sense that matters, cannot be taught. It can only be learned, and learned by each separate one of us in his own way, by the use of his own powers of imagination and perception, the ability to learn the lessons he has set for himself.

The Collected Essays and Occasional Writings of
Katherine Anne Porter: On Writing

You finally do have to give something terribly intimate and secret of yourself to the world and not care, because you have to believe that what you have to say is important enough.

May Sarton: A Self-Portrait

We shall not create original or productive art by the chance encounter of passing emotions whose image we may reproduce more or less faithfully, but by giving ourselves for what we are and seeking to be worth much in order that we may give much.

JEANNE DE VIETINGHOFF: *The Understanding of Good*

So long as you write what you wish to write, that is all that matters; and whether it matters for ages or only for hours, nobody can say. But to sacrifice a hair of the head of your vision, a shade of its colour, in deference to some Headmaster with a silver pot in his hand or to some professor with a measuring-rod up his sleeve, is the most abject treachery, and the sacrifice of wealth and chastity which used to be said to be the greatest of human disasters, a mere flea-bite in comparison.

VIRGINIA WOOLF: *A Room of One's Own*

Moreover, it is all very well for you, who have got yourselves to college and enjoy sitting-rooms of your own to say that genius should disregard opinions; that genius should be above caring what is said of it. Unfortunately, it is precisely the men or women of genius who mind most what is said of them. Remember Keats. Remember the words he had cut on his tombstone. Think of Tennyson; think—but I need hardly multiply instances of the undeniable, if very unfortunate fact that it is the nature of the artist to mind excessively what is said about him. Literature is strewn with the wreckage of men who have minded beyond reason the opinions of others.

VIRGINIA WOOLF: *A Room of One's Own*

Sometimes the business part of writing grows very noxious to me, and I wonder if in heaven our best thoughts—poets' thoughts, especially—will not be flowers, somehow, or some sort of beautiful live things that stand about and grow, and don't have to be chaffered over and bought and sold. It seems as bad as selling our fellow beings.

The Letters of Sarah Orne Jewett

X asked me whether it was difficult or easy to write poetry. I answered that when somebody dictates it to you, it's easy, but that when there is nobody dictating—it's quite impossible.

ANNA AKHMATOVA: *My Half Century*

To be a poet is to have a soul so quick to discern, that no shade of quality escapes it, and so quick to feel, that discernment is but a hand playing with finely ordered variety on the chords of emotion—a soul in which knowledge passes instantaneously into feeling, and feeling flashes back as a new organ of knowledge. One may have that condition by fits only.

GEORGE ELIOT: *Middlemarch*

At its best, the sensation of writing is that of any unmerited grace. It is handed to you, but only if you look for it. You search, you break your heart, your back, your brain, and then— and only then—it is handed to you.

ANNIE DILLARD: *The Writing Life*

Nobody whispers it in your ear. It is like something you memorized once and forgot. Now it comes back and rips away your breath. You find and finger a phrase at a time; you lay it down cautiously, as if with tongs, and wait suspended until the next one finds you.

ANNIE DILLARD: *The Writing Life*

The sensation of writing a book is the sensation of spinning, blinded by love and daring. It is the sensation of rearing and peering from the bent tip of a grassblade, looking for a route.

ANNIE DILLARD: *The Writing Life*

How many moments have I lost—if I can call them lost—with flowers as avid for moisture as the anemone, the tulip, the hyacinth, the wild orchid! Swooning with heat and thirst, their stalks, plunged into water, imbibe so much, so greedily, that the energetic movement of the flower, its return to the vertical, become visible, jerky at first and by fits and starts when the head is too rich and too heavy. It is a pleasure sweet to a writer to witness the rebirth of a tulip in a crystal goblet. The ink dries on the pen while before me a creation, interrupted by a transient death, raises itself toward perfection and will attain it, shine for a day, perish the next . . .

COLETTE: *Journey for Myself*

Letting go
in order to hold on
I gradually understand
how poems are made.

There is a place the fear must go.
There is a place the choice must go.
There is a place the loss must go.
The leftover love.
The love that spills out
of the too full cup
and runs and hides
its too full self
in shame.

I gradually comprehend
how poems are made.
To the upbeat flight of memories.
The flagged beats of the running
heart.

ALICE WALKER: *"How Poems Are Made: A Discredited View"*

It would be a thousand pities if women wrote like men, or lived like men, or looked like men, for if two sexes are quite inadequate, considering the vastness and variety of the world, how should we manage with one only! Ought not education to bring out and fortify the differences rather than the similarities? For we have too much likeness as it is.

VIRGINIA WOOLF: *A Room of One's Own*

Male and female represent the two sides of the great radical dualism. But, in fact, they are perpetually passing into one another. Fluid hardens into solid, solid rushes to fluid. There is no wholly masculine man, no purely feminine woman.

MARGARET FULLER: *Woman in the Nineteenth Century*

By accepting both the masculine and feminine principles in their entirety and with all their differences, each one's essentialness to the other will be recognized and a new whole will be freed to emerge. This new whole will be more complex than anything that has existed until now. It will have an entirely new dimension.

Men would in fact be helping women if they re-claimed that wild man aspect of themselves, that particularly masculine essence which they are in danger of losing through trying to conform to an inappropriate image of what some contemporary women say they want men to be. They would enable the women to start discovering the next stage of the true feminine, which is beyond the whole question of subjection and domination and inequality. This in turn would give them access to the true masculine in themselves.

The archetype of the feminine has in this age been very overshadowed by the mother archetype. So powerful and uppermost has she become, that other aspects of the feminine have to some extent been lost. Emphasis must be taken away from the mother and given to that special feminine catalytic power which is so essential to all creativity.

GILDAS (CHANNELED THROUGH RUTH WHITE):
Sexuality & Spirituality

Truly, every new idea is a violation of some older idea; as the awakening of tomorrow is a violation of today's slumber. As long as man continues to evolve, in other words, to separate himself from chaos, and to express himself in a higher form, he must always shatter something. In shattering, he disobeys; in breaking, he creates.

Jeanne de Vietinghoff: *The Understanding of Good*

The earth is in many senses a manifestation of the feminine. If the journey of the feminine is neglected, the planet will become even more sick than she already is. When the call of her feminine unconscious is responded to, a solution will be found. This is beginning through your growing concern for ecology. With the active involvement in restoring the earth's feminine energy and creativity, there lies great hope.

Gildas (channeled through Ruth White): *Sexuality & Spirituality*

I shall devote only a few lines to the expression of my belief in the importance of science . . . it is by this daily striving after knowledge that man has raised himself to the unique position he occupies on earth, and that his power and well-being have continually increased. We in our Committee should be among those who, with Rodin, bow before the toilsome effort of the thinker, and who with Pasteur, "never doubt but that knowledge and peace will triumph over ignorance and war." Indeed, if the mentality of the scholars of the various countries, as revealed by the recent war, often appears to be on the lower level than that of the less cultured masses, it is because there is a danger inherent in all power that is not disciplined and directed towards the higher aims which alone are worthy of it. Thus no movement can be more important than those which have for their object the forging of international links among the most active thinking minds, and more particularly among the members of the younger generation, on whom the future depends.

Memorandum by Madame Curie, Member of the Committee,
League of Nations, Committee on Intellectual Cooperation:
International Scholarships for the Advancement of the Sciences, 1926

There should, I think, be basic courses at a very simple level, which would teach children that they are living in the midst of the universe on a planet whose resources they will one day need to conserve, that they depend on the air and the water and on all living creatures, and that the slightest error or act of violence could possibly destroy everything. They would learn that men have killed one another in wars that have never done anything but lead to other wars, and that every country doctors its history to make itself look good. They would learn enough about the past to feel a bond to the men and women who have gone before them and to admire where admiration is due, but without setting up idols; nor should there be idols for today or for any hypothetical tomorrow. Some effort should be devoted to familiarizing the children with both books and things. They should know the names of plants and should be taught about animals . . .

MARGUERITE YOURCENAR: *With Open Eyes*

I think it is important to have some notion of what life is like when encased in a form different from our own. For us it's a major step forward to realize that the form we happen to be accustomed to living in is not the only one in which life dwells;

life can come with wings instead of arms, with eyes more acute than ours, with gills instead of lungs. Then there are the mysteries of animal migration and communication; there is the intelligence of certain species—the dolphin, for example, is our equal in brainpower, though its image of the world is surely different from ours . . .

. . . They should learn how to give first aid to the injured . . . Teachers would also instill the simple ethical ideas without which life in society is impossible, something that elementary and middle schools in the United States no longer dare to attempt. In religion, no practice or dogma would be imposed, but something would be said about all of the world's great religions, and particularly about those prevalent locally, in order to kindle respect for religion in the child's mind and to eliminate certain hateful prejudices . . .

MARGUERITE YOURCENAR: *With Open Eyes*

What one believes matters little, what matters is *how* one believes.
JEANNE DE VIETINGHOFF: *The Understanding of Good*

Children should be taught to love work, provided it is useful.
MARGUERITE YOURCENAR: *With Open Eyes*

No human pursuit achieves dignity until it can be called work.
BERYL MARKHAM: *West with the Night*

The worth of a human creature will always depend on the cost he is prepared to pay; and his progress will be proportionate to the strength of his effort.

JEANNE DE VIETINGHOFF: *The Understanding of Good*

It always seems to me more and more that the only thing that really matters in life is not wealth or poverty, pleasure or hardship, but the nature of the human beings with whom one is thrown into contact and one's relation to them. One's real deathless wealth is all the beautiful noble souls one has seen and spiritually touched.

The Letters of Olive Schreiner

From all the offspring
of the earth and heaven
love is the most precious

SAPPHO: a fragment

What I am proposing would be, for the first time in history, a humane education.

MARGUERITE YOURCENAR: *With Open Eyes*

It may be there is no other way of educating people. Possibly, but I don't believe it. In the meantime it would be a help at least to describe things properly, to call things by their right names. Ideally, what should be said to every child, repeatedly, throughout his or her school life is something like this: "You are in the process of being indoctrinated. We have not yet evolved a system of education that is not a system of indoctrination. We are sorry, but it is the best we can do. What you are being taught here is an amalgam of current prejudice and the choices of this particular culture. The slightest look at history will show how impermanent these must be. You are being taught by people who have been able to accommodate themselves to a regime of thought laid down by their predecessors. It is a self-perpetuating system. Those of you who are more robust and individual than others, will be encouraged to leave and find ways of educating yourself—educating your own judgment. Those who stay must remember, always and all the time, that they are being molded and patterned to fit into the narrow and particular needs of this particular society."

DORIS LESSING: *Preface to The Golden Notebook*

As in the political sphere, the child is taught that he is free, a democrat, with a free will and a free mind, lives in a free country, makes his own decisions. At the same time he is a prisoner of the assumptions and dogmas of his time, which he does not question, because he has never been told they exist. By the time a young person has reached the age when he has to choose (we still take it for granted that a choice is inevitable) between the arts and the sciences, he often chooses the arts because he feels that here is humanity, freedom, choice. He does not know that he is already molded by a system: he does not know that the choice itself is the result of a false dichotomy rooted in the heart of our culture. Those who do sense this, and who don't wish to subject themselves to further molding, tend to leave, in a half-unconscious, instinctive attempt to find work where they won't be divided against themselves. With all our institutions, from the police force to academia, from medicine to politics, we give little attention to the people who leave—that process of elimination that goes on all the time and which excludes, very early, those likely to be original and reforming, leaving those attracted to a thing because that is what they are already like . . . These children who have spent years inside the training system become critics and reviewers, and cannot give what the author, the artist, so foolishly looks for—imaginative and original judgment.

DORIS LESSING: *Preface to The Golden Notebook*

Not by measuring our knowledge, but by admitting the grandeur of the unknowable and telling ourselves that we depend entirely on it, shall we attain the full amplitude of our soul and the greatest measure of justice in our life.

JEANNE DE VIETINGHOFF: *The Understanding of Good*

Remember that for all the books we have in print, there are as many that have never reached print, have never been written down. Even now, in this age of compulsive reverence for the written word, history, even social ethic, are taught by means of stories, and the people who have been conditioned into thinking only in terms of what is written—and unfortunately nearly all the products of our educational system can do no more than this—are missing what is before their eyes. For instance, the real history of Africa is still in the custody of black storytellers and wise men, black historians, medicine men: it is a verbal history, still kept safe from the white man and his predations. Everywhere, if you keep your mind open, you will find the truth in words *not* written down. So never let the printed page be your master . . . you should be learning to follow your own intuitive feeling about what you need.

DORIS LESSING: *Preface to The Golden Notebook*

Just as appearing beings living in a world of appearances have an urge to show themselves, so thinking beings, which still belong to the world of appearances even after they have mentally withdrawn from it, have an urge to speak and thus to make manifest what otherwise would not be a part of the appearing world at all.

HANNAH ARENDT: *The Life of the Mind*

It is not that in my pride I want to suggest that I am isolated by my opinions in this world only because of my exceptional greatness or intelligence. No! I am a creature riddled with faults and weaknesses, and the thickest veils of ignorance shroud my mind's brightest insights. I am alone as a result of disenchantment and lost illusions. Those illusions were palpable; but who has not been taken in by them? They were shattered; who has not also seen his own turn to dust? But there was one I had in particular, vast and beautiful, such as my soul was in those early years when I had just emerged from adolescence. That one proved to be a seal of everlasting calamity, a death sentence. But all this would require a great deal more space and a kind of history of my youth.

GEORGE SAND: *Lettres d'un voyageur*

The companions of our childhood always possess a certain power over our minds which hardly any later friend can obtain. They know our infantine dispositions which however they may be afterwards modified, are never eradicated.

MARY SHELLEY: *Frankenstein*

No matter how far away you are, I see you still,
No matter how far away you are, you still remain—
Like a presence that will never fade,
Like the landscape of my life.

LOU ANDREAS-SALOME: *Looking Back*

What a bad joke the human heart is.

GEORGE SAND: *Lettres d'un voyageur*

I feel at times I understand love, in the end I can never really explain it.

TING LING: *I Myself Am a Woman*

Love is real: the most real, the most lasting—the sweetest and yet the bitterest thing we know.

An Hour with Charlotte Brontë

. . . like all truly mystical things, love is rooted deeply and rightly in this world and this flesh. This phase is natural, dangerous but not necessarily fatal; so remarkably educational it would be a great pity to miss it; further, of great importance, for the flesh in real love is one of the many bridges to the spirit; still, a phase only, which being passed is too often mistaken for the whole thing, and the end of it. This is an error based on lack of imagination, or the simple incapacity for further and deeper exploration of life, there being always on hand great numbers of people who are unwilling or unable to grow up, no matter what happens to them.

The Collected Essays and Occasional Writings of Katherine Anne Porter: Marriage Is Belonging

Love opens the doors into everything as far as I can see, including and perhaps most of all, the door into one's own secret and often terribly frightening, real self.

May Sarton: A Self-Portrait

If another woman were to ask my advice about spending her life so much alone as I have done I should say NO. You feel the knocks the world gives you too much, because there is nothing to stand between you and the world . . . you can feel the blows come straight on the bone.

The Letters of Olive Schreiner

I've had such a happy day working . . . People think I have a lonely life, but I believe I'm the happiest person in the world; whether my work is artistic or scientific I feel as if I were in heaven when I am absolutely in it. The terrible part is to think I will ever have to publish it.

The Letters of Olive Schreiner

I am very happy in my work, but I wish the Gods would give me three hundred years to live instead of a few score.

The Letters of Olive Schreiner

Only when one is connected to one's own core is one connected to others I am beginning to discover. And, for me, the core, the inner spring, can best be refound through solitude.

ANNE MORROW LINDBERGH: *Gift from the Sea*

One thing is beautiful to me, that though my personal life has become crushed and indifferent to me, I have not lost one little grain of my faith in the possible beauty and greatness of human nature, the divine beauty of perfect love, and of truth.

The Letters of Olive Schreiner

If the beauty I see in my hours of solitude ravishes my soul, my rapture will be more intense when it is shared, and I shall never create better than when I do so for the love of some human creature and under the influence of that love.

JEANNE DE VIETINGHOFF: *The Understanding of Good*

For no science, no ambition, no joy can replace that marvelous unfolding which true love brings to the soul.

JEANNE DE VIETINGHOFF: *The Understanding of Good*

And the soul that has not found its complement continues to seek by instinct and without halt. In youth we seek it in passion. This is why love, for so many simply a fortuitous circumstance, is for others life itself.

JEANNE DE VIETINGHOFF: *The Understanding of Good*

The misty nights of our temperate provinces have charms which no one has appreciated more than I have nor is less ready to deny. Here nature, with its more vigorous impact, tends to impose perhaps too much silence on the mind. It inhibits thought, perturbs the heart and dominates the senses. No one but a genius should think of writing during those voluptuous nights: they are for love or sleep.

GEORGE SAND: *Lettres d'un voyageur*

I seem to drink in the external world through every little pore . . . seem conscious of nothing but an all-powerful desire to drink in through my senses.

The Letters of Olive Schreiner

Without warning
As a whirlwind
swoops on an oak
Love shakes my heart

SAPPHO: a fragment

What is the mystery of passion, spiritually speaking? For there is a passion of the spirit. Blind passion, as it has most truly been called, seems to come on in man without his exactly knowing why, without his at all knowing why for this person rather than for that, and (whether it has been satisfied or unsatisfied) to go off again after a while, as it came, also without his knowing why.

FLORENCE NIGHTINGALE: *Cassandra*

What is that electricity they speak of, whose changes make us well or ill; whose lack or excess blasts; whose even balance revives? What are all those influences that are about us in the atmosphere, that keep playing over our nerves like fingers on stringed instruments, and call forth now a sweet note, and now a wail—now an exultant swell, and anon the saddest cadence?

An Hour with Charlotte Brontë

What is this heart we talk about so much and so well? What makes it so whimsical, so inconsistent, so reluctant to suffer, so willing to rejoice? Is there a good and a bad angel who take it in turns to breathe upon this miserable life-giving organ? Can this diaphragm, which expands in response to a cup of coffee and a kind word, be a spirit, a spark of Divinity? But if it is nothing but a blood-soaked sponge where do these sudden aspirations, these tremors come from? How can anguish suddenly burst from it in harrowing cries when certain syllables reach our ears, or when a lamp, playing on the fringe of a curtain . . . throws on the wall some fantastic silhouettes, some profiles sketched by chance, stamped with uncanny resemblances? What is it that makes some of us, in the middle of our dinner parties—where, thank God, there is no lack of noise and merriment—begin to sob without knowing why?

GEORGE SAND: *Lettres d'un Voyageur*

It is truly a suffering that has no name, no meaning, no clear purpose—a suffering without truce and without end, which one endures, not because of the evil one has been guilty of, but through the virtue one has made one's own.

JEANNE DE VIETINGHOFF: *The Understanding of Good*

Belief in happiness is not an illusion of youth, as is often assumed, but the experience of a force that grows and triumphs over reality. The more our feeble hope is flung and broken against the deceptions of life, the more surely will it rise powerful and transformed.

JEANNE DE VIETINGHOFF: *The Understanding of Good*

For the higher natures, whose tastes and habits have been turned from childhood towards the beautiful, and who believe in the possibility of realizing their inner ideals, resignation is more painful; a disappointment is always a disturbing problem to them, and may even appear to be an irretrievable disaster.

JEANNE DE VIETINGHOFF: *The Understanding of Good*

The craving for happiness is an instinct as ineradicable as it is necessary; therefore we ought to understand it and cultivate it as a sacred gift confided to man by God.

JEANNE DE VIETINGHOFF: *The Understanding of Good*

The deadly shock arising from the encounter of the highest conception with brutal realities is the supreme injustice, for it is the chastisement of good. But it is only at the price of this long death of starvation that the spirit can triumph, even as the flower can only unfold through the withering of its sheath.

JEANNE DE VIETINGHOFF: *The Understanding of Good*

. . . just as the ugly caterpillar is the beginning of the splendid butterfly, this globe is the embryo of a new heaven and of a new earth whose meagerest beauty infinitely surpasses mortal imagination.

EMILY BRONTË: *Five Essays Written in French, The Butterfly*

Throughout the centuries there were men who took first steps down new roads armed with nothing but their own vision. Their goals differed, but they all had this in common: that the step was first, the road new, the vision unborrowed, and the response they received—hatred. The great creators—the thinkers, the artists, the scientists, the inventors—stood alone against the men of their time. Every great new thought was opposed. Every great new invention was denounced. But the men of unborrowed vision went ahead. They fought, they suffered and they paid. But they won . . .

His truth was his only motive. His own truth, and his own work to achieve it in his own way. A symphony, a book, an engine, a philosophy, an airplane or a building—that was his goal and his life. The creation gave form to his truth. He held his truth above all things and against all men. His vision, his strength, his courage came from his own spirit. That entity which is his consciousness.

AYN RAND: *The Soul of an Individualist* from *For the New Intellectual*

As vast and incomprehensible in its ultimate nature as light or time, or space, or matter generally, is that other vast reality which we know and feel more intimately than anything else in the universe, the will within us that is not time nor space, that is not light nor heat; incomprehensible in its ultimate essence by our puny intellects as is everything else in the universe, yet never for a moment to be ignored if we do not wish to wreck our lives and make a fool's play of our existence.

The Letters of Olive Schreiner

In order to avoid the contagion of lies and recover our true nature—that nature lying at the core of every heart, though few will admit it—we must have the courage to see ourselves as we really are. We must, if only for a moment, cast off all the exigencies of life, religious and moral obligations and alien influences—the artifice we mistake for our veritable self and believe necessary to our well-being, while in reality it is our chief hindrance.

JEANNE DE VIETINGHOFF: *The Understanding of Good*

Do we really owe our progress to the conquests of our thought? Is there not a force more real, more stable, in the depths of our soul, which stands for our true greatness and on which we truly lean?

JEANNE DE VIETINGHOFF: *The Understanding of Good*

Though it is in no way dependent on our impulses or actions, all our life depends on it; for it is the force that in all our victories or defeats ceases not to urge us forward; and it is surely because we count on this mysterious asset that even in the vortex of our most ignominious failures we will not surrender.

JEANNE DE VIETINGHOFF: *The Understanding of Good*

It is, after all, of small importance if our inferior self is victor or vanquished in this strange crisis we call life, for how can real tragedy touch a being whose humiliation is transient and whose triumph is ephemeral?

JEANNE DE VIETINGHOFF: *The Understanding of Good*

Real transgression is an unseen, profound and infinitely subtle act that happens in the secret place of our being; it is a falsehood of the soul, a wrong we do, not to others, but to ourselves. We are guilty of it every time we disobey what we have recognized as being the best and highest in us.

JEANNE DE VIETINGHOFF: *The Understanding of Good*

The secret instinct, named in turn intuition, inspiration, grace, by morality, art and religion, remains the greatest, the most real and possibly the only immortal part of us.

JEANNE DE VIETINGHOFF: *The Understanding of Good*

It is an immortal temple rising in the midst of all that is transient, which abides when all else is gone, which promises us the continuance of that which we are and the plenitude of that which we shall one day be!

JEANNE DE VIETINGHOFF: *The Understanding of Good*

It is the instrument of progress and the truth of the future—that truth which must prevail against all the conquests of force, reason and intelligence.

JEANNE DE VIETINGHOFF: *The Understanding of Good*

It is part of the unceasing human endeavor to prove that the spirit of man can transcend the flaws of his own nature.

AUNG SAN SUU KYI: *Freedom from Fear*

It is because of this tendency to use my brain as a magnifying glass that I have always, at first, found reality small and lacking in grandeur. It has taken time to accept it without contempt and, finally, to find in it specific beauties and things to admire other than those I sought.

GEORGE SAND: *Lettres d'un voyageur*

Not by dreaming, pondering or conjecturing about life can we learn to know it, but by living it, and it is through our collision with reality that we prove our grain.

JEANNE DE VIETINGHOFF: *The Understanding of Good*

Yet I still love to adorn reality, however beautiful it may be. Such a tendency denotes neither the artist nor the poet, I know; it denotes the madman.

GEORGE SAND: *Lettres d'un voyageur*

Much Madness is divinest Sense—
To a discerning Eye—
Much Sense—the starkest Madness—
'Tis the Majority
In this, as All, prevail—
Assent—and you are sane—
Demur—you're straightway dangerous
And handled with a Chain—

The Poems of Emily Dickinson

As it happens, the issues that concern and upset me have as yet captured the interest of only a minority of my compatriots, but I believe that these issues will become increasingly important as time goes by . . . the destruction of the planet by air and water pollution; the extinction of whole species, which is tipping the vital equilibrium between humans and the environment; the confrontation of each of us with himself and with God (however that word be interpreted) . . .

MARGUERITE YOURCENAR: *With Open Eyes*

I have some long and tall thoughts on the subject of God's working through nature, but I will not inflict them on you now.

Letters of Flannery O'Connor: The Habit of Being

We in the "developed" world seem to have many auditory strategies that insulate us from the presence of silence, simplicity, and solitude. When I return to Western culture after time in desert, mountain, or forest, I discover how we have filled our world with a multiplicity of noises, a symphony of forgetfulness that keeps our own thoughts and realizations, feelings and intuitions out of audible range ... The sound of suffering is covered over by the ceaseless song of longing for more; the mindless tunes of elevator music; the crackling of "news"; the grind of transiting vehicles ... the remorseless electrical hum and whir tuning us to the shared frequency of the developed world ... Time in our culture is scheduled to the minute lest we "have time on our hands." The television set, the electronic hearth, holds young and old in a time trance ... We fill our homes and our offices with "things" and "more things," and the overflow finds its way into crowded storage lockers ...

JOAN HALIFAX: *The Fruitful Darkness*

I was told the brown falcon that continued to follow us reminded the people that sometimes we believe in what we see immediately ahead of us.

MARLO MORGAN: *Mutant Message Down Under*

When we begin to have a sense of the fabricated nature of who we are in the social or relative sense, we commonly experience a crisis. We often create another social role to make ourselves feel secure. We put on another hat, find another job, change religions or relationships.

JOAN HALIFAX: *The Fruitful Darkness*

Oblivion is a stupid monster that has devoured too many generations ... Escape oblivion ...

GEORGE SAND: *Histoire de ma vie*

People need to relearn how to love the human condition as it is, to accept its limitations and its dangers, to take a hard look at things as they are.

MARGUERITE YOURCENAR: *With Open Eyes*

If we only lift ourselves and soar higher, we can see a view where a much bigger picture is taking place.

MARLO MORGAN: *Mutant Message Down Under*

It is a vast universal truth that is present around us every-where . . .

(Humans do not, on the whole, understand the dynamic relationship between spirit and matter. Nature does. It is the dynamic which is inherent within the life force of nature.)
—the Overlighting Deva of Perelandra

MACHAELLE SMALL WRIGHT:
Behaving As If The God In All Life Mattered

If we look deeply we find that we do not have a separate self, a self that does not include sun and wind, earth and water, creatures and plants, and one another.

MARGUERITE YOURCENAR: *With Open Eyes*

The truth is, all life is one life . . . It is all one, our ancestors, our unborn grandchildren, all of life everywhere . . .

MARLO MORGAN: *Mutant Message Down Under*

All humanity and all of life course through our veins, and if their ceaseless flow happens to have chosen the path of a particular family and society, the one in which one happens to have grown up, that is just one accident among many that shape one's life.

MARGUERITE YOURCENAR: With Open Eyes

Our true identity . . . a deeper identity . . . beyond our psycho-social one . . . is about relationship and process, and also empty of any distinctions and free of boundaries or qualities of separateness.

JOAN HALIFAX: The Fruitful Darkness

Every relation, every gradation of nature is incalculably precious, but only to the soul which is poised upon itself, and to whom no loss, no change, can bring dull discord, for it is in harmony with the central soul.

MARGARET FULLER: Woman in the Nineteenth Century

Each of us has more power over the world than we imagine.

MARGUERITE YOURCENAR: With Open Eyes

To live! What heroism that word stands for! To live! Compared with the effort life demands, death seems but the idle game of a child. Resignation may have its justification; it is but human, since we are weak and surrounded by enemies. But to blossom forth in gladness is superhuman; it is to contradict evidence, to affirm the unknowable, to will the impossible. Many may teach us how to die: God alone can sometimes enable us to live.

JEANNE DE VIETINGHOFF: The Understanding of Good

Two or three people, with healthy bodies and the right sort of receiving brains, could turn the whole tide of human thought, could direct lightning flashes of electric power to slash across and destroy the world of dead, murky thought. Two or three people gathered together in the name of truth, beauty, and over-mind consciousness could bring the whole force of this power back into the world.

H.D. (HILDA DOOLITTLE): *Notes on Thought and Vision*

What a man may do, each soul, is to exert a tiny influence in the direction good and beautiful to him; and then he dies peaceful, having attained his end, whether it be making fairer one soul, waking one impulse of tenderness and love in another soul, painting a picture, discovering a beautiful sequence in events, and realizing the reason in the nature of the universe, and showing it to others as all true scientific discoverers do.

The Letters of Olive Schreiner

We must endeavor to leave behind us a world a little cleaner, a little more beautiful than it was, even if that world extends no farther than our backyard or kitchen.

MARGUERITE YOURCENAR: *With Open Eyes*

I shall never be a mathematician, nor a man of science making vast discoveries, nor a great leader of people bound to them in love and sympathy and giving them voices . . . a mother devoting myself entirely to the joy of bearing, rearing my children . . . I shall never find out if I have the power for music I have always felt I have, shall never know that craving to paint I have had since I was a little child . . . in my poor little handful of life . . . I shall know few things . . . but this I have . . .

The Letters of Olive Schreiner

... a full, adult, living, breathing life in close contact with what I love—the earth and the wonders thereof—the sea—the sun ... I want to enter into it, to be part of it, to live in it, to learn from it, to lose all that is superficial and acquired in me and to become a conscious direct human being. I want, by understanding myself, to understand others. I want to be all that I am capable of becoming so that I may be (and here I have stopped and waited and waited and it's no good—there's only one phrase that will do) a child of the sun. About helping others, about carrying a light and so on, it seems false to say a single word. Let it be at that. A child of the sun ...

And out of this, the expression of this, I want to be writing.

The Journal of Katherine Mansfield

I must speak by such means as are within my reach.

JANE AUSTEN: *Persuasion*

I have just had a new wonderful idea for a wild story. Not at all like my usual ones, but it will be splendid when I am able to write it. The idea is the conscious transmigration of a soul. A wild weird impossible thing, real of course—the feeling.

The Letters of Olive Schreiner

Truth can never be cheaply bought. As soon as the soul seeks to substantiate its true essence, it must be prepared to accept defeat and privation. But, in the teeth of this defeat, the spiritual man breaks his bonds and forges a passage towards a larger future, a fuller destiny.

JEANNE DE VIETINGHOFF: *The Understanding of Good*

The soul, awakening, finds itself faced by three possibilities: resignation of its ideal, thereby accepting the current mediocrity; creation of an illusory ideal by refusing to see things as they are; or to risk being crushed through remaining faithful to itself and appraising mankind at its true value. Only a really pure soul seems capable of confronting this cruel contradiction; and this, not from inclination or a sense of duty, but because it is constrained by its very nature to prefer death to the loss of its ideal . . .

As life is in the plant, so is good in us, and it will speed us, when we have once surrendered ourselves to its power, through all the joyous or disturbing fluctuations of existence, towards the fulfillment of our supreme destiny . . .

JEANNE DE VIETINGHOFF: *The Understanding of Good*

Certain beings are purer than others because, having been in conflict with evil, they have suffered more for the sake of good. A truly pure life is one that, fully cognizant of reality, has known how to surmount it.

JEANNE DE VIETINGHOFF: *The Understanding of Good*

Good in the heart of man can only advance with a slow and almost imperceptible motion. Our intellect may conceive an ideal, our will may strive after it, but to live it we must wait patiently till our soul shall have acquired the force, the greatness and the purity necessary for its realization.

JEANNE DE VIETINGHOFF: *The Understanding of Good*

The spirit demands more than established order.

JEANNE DE VIETINGHOFF: *The Understanding of Good*

The spirit demands something more than unconscious contentment.

JEANNE DE VIETINGHOFF: *The Understanding of Good*

Nothing is so personal as happiness; each soul is fitted for a joy entirely individual; often a whole life is required to discover it.

JEANNE DE VIETINGHOFF: *The Understanding of Good*

In the spiritual, as in the material realm, one must dare in order to succeed: dare to see, to believe, to doubt, to love, to suffer and to be.

JEANNE DE VIETINGHOFF: *The Understanding of Good*

To vibrate, to accept, to expand—this is the new duty; to give oneself as one is, to let life meet us as it really is, to live for the moment and extract from each moment all that it holds of truth, beauty and goodness, without scruple or arriere-pensee, without vain questioning, in the spontaneous desire of life, in childlike purity of heart; to be able to be oneself, to dare to be happy and at last allow one's soul to spread its wings and mount to God in a natural and impulsive ardour. . . .

JEANNE DE VIETINGHOFF: *The Understanding of Good*

To pass beyond the zone of tribulation and the sickness of scruples; to be capable of facing all, free to accept all; to have faith in one's own heart, and to give as the heart dictates; for the sincere heart is also pure.

To will no more—for to will is to impose a direction on destiny—but to let ourselves be led where fate will, even were the path not that of our desire; for life is everywhere, happiness in all things, it is we who create them.

JEANNE DE VIETINGHOFF: *The Understanding of Good*

True happiness is not to be found outside life; it does not brood above as the sky broods over the earth; it is in life, it is life itself—full life with all its heroic struggles and sublime joys.

JEANNE DE VIETINGHOFF: *The Understanding of Good*

My poem, as I look at it this morning is not so good as I hoped. It began well and may end well, but there is a long way to go . . .

The Collected Essays and Occasional Writings of Katherine Anne Porter: Notes on Writing

I am now and then haunted by some semi-mystic very profound life of a woman, which shall all be told on one occasion; and time shall be obliterated; future shall somehow blossom out of the past. One incident—say the fall of a flower—might contain it. My theory being that the actual event practically does not exist—nor time either. But I don't want to force this . . . I want to watch and see how the idea at first occurs. I want to trace my own process . . .

VIRGINIA WOOLF: *A Writer's Diary*

But what is to become of all these diaries, I asked myself yesterday . . . I daresay there is a little book in them; if the scraps and scratching were straightened out a little. God knows.

VIRGINIA WOOLF: *A Writer's Diary*

I did have a moment of quiet panic at how much of me has been given away. But I decided that one does not lose one's soul for giving it away.

May Sarton: A Self-Portrait

The Price of My Soul refers not to the price for which I would be prepared to sell out, but rather to the price we all must pay in life to preserve our own integrity. To gain that which is worth having it may be necessary to lose everything else.

BERNADETTE DEVLIN: *The Price of My Soul*

I really only ask for time to write it all—time to write my books. Then I don't mind dying. I live to write. The lovely world (God how lovely the external world is!) is there and I bathe in it and am refreshed. But I feel as though I had a duty, someone has set me a task which I am bound to finish. Let me finish it without hurrying, leaving all as fair as I can . . .

The Journal of Katherine Mansfield

I want so to live that I work with my hands and my feeling and my brain. I want a garden, a small house, grass, animals, books, pictures, music. And out of this, the expression of this, I want to be writing . . . But warm, eager, living life—to be rooted in life—to learn, to desire to know, to feel, to think, to act. That is what I want. And nothing less. That is what I must try for.

The Journal of Katherine Mansfield

If my books are read, if they reach one person, a single one, and help that person in some way, if only for an instant, I consider myself useful. Furthermore, since I believe that all our impulses endure forever, just as all things continue to survive in one form or another, this usefulness can perpetuate itself indefinitely. A book may lie dormant for fifty years or for two thousand years in a forgotten corner of a library, only to reveal, upon being opened, the marvels or the abysses that it contains, or the line that seems to have been written for me alone. In this respect the writer is not different from any other human being: whatever we say or do can have far-reaching consequences. We must endeavor to leave behind us a world a little cleaner, a little more beautiful than it was . . .

MARGUERITE YOURCENAR: *With Open Eyes*

This is not a part I am playing, it is not a duty, it is not even calculated; it is an instinct and a need . . . Write your own history, all of you who have understood your life and sounded your heart . . . to that end alone I am writing my own.

GEORGE SAND: *Histoire de ma vie*

Note to the Actress

(and an infusion of Gertrude Stein)

ecause *The Words of a Woman* is composed entirely of excerpts from great literature—literature that had already been excerpted, edited, and intertwined—it would have been unthinkable to further interrupt it with stage direction. Dramatic presentation of the piece is entrusted to the magic of theatre and to a gifted actress and director.

The following is a Gertrude Stein passage, which was too special to be left out but which begged the company of stage direction. It creates an opportunity for the actress to get up from the desk and draw her audience into her writing room (which may be embellished with bookcases full of books, warm draperies, a comfortable chair for reading, etc.). This bit of text may also be inserted in a simple theatrical setting where the actress simply reaches for the book that sits among the other books next to her, on the top of her desk:

After the words "For so many people, love seems to be simply a fortuitous circumstance. For others it is life itself," she looks off into the distance where she remains for a time, and then, as if to rescue herself from her last words, she utters another. She announces it as though she were letting it loose into the universe for the very first time: "Romance." She meditates for a moment, remembering something. What was that passage? she thinks to herself. She gets up from the desk, goes to the bookshelf, and begins scanning the books, repeating the word aloud—"romance, romance"—as though thumbing through the Yellow Pages. She grabs Gertrude Stein's *The Geographical History of America* and begins leafing through it as she comes back to her desk. She has an idea of just the location of the passage, somewhere near the middle on the left-hand page; she has retained a picture of it. She comes across something she can not resist; she reads it aloud:

"The human mind has what it has does what it does and writes what it writes and that has nothing to do with identity or audience or history or events, and yet only once in every few generations the human mind writes. That is all because of human nature and human nature is not interesting everybody says it is but it is not."

She is pleased and amused and nourished, remembering how much she enjoys Stein's presentation. She flips the page and continues scanning; she reads another passage aloud: "Every once in so often is every once in so often and anybody can decide what nothing is." And in another moment, "Think what the human mind is." Her eyes continue traveling down the page, and then as if she were saying Aha!, "Romance!" She has found it. She reads loudly and resolutely:

"Romance. There is some relation between romance and the human mind but no relation between human nature and romantic anything because human nature is not interesting but *romance* is."

She smiles with great satisfaction. She stretches her lower back from one side to the other. She is still trying to avoid her earlier thought of love being for some people absolute life itself. Stein has not distracted her. She is physically possessed by the night. She finally speaks directly to her feeling. (Back to the text.) "No one but a *genius* should think of writing on misty, voluptuous nights!"

The literature abounds with opportunity for a rich theatrical experience.

Be true to the words and they will be your guide.

Words
About the Women

Anna Akhmatova (1889–1966)

RUSSIAN POET

Anna Akhmatova was praised at her death as the greatest female poet in Russian literature—acclaim which emerged in stark contrast to the criticism, oppression, and ostracism she endured during her life under the Stalin regime. Her poetry was repeatedly banned and destroyed, resurfacing at one point only to suffer the indignity of glorifying Stalin and Soviet Communism in order to win her son's release from Siberian exile. This agonizing humiliation was in vain, and at her request these poems were not included in her later collected works. Anna Akhmatova, condemned for her narrow preoccupation with love and God, outlived her persecutors. In her later years she was awarded the Etna-Taonmina International Poetry Prize as well as an honorary degree from Oxford University. A literary heroine of the Russian people, she is regarded throughout the world as one of the great poets of the twentieth century.

Lou Andreas-Salome (1861–1937)

GERMAN AUTHOR

Lou Andreas-Salome is known primarily because her life was intertwined with the lives of two of the most important thinkers of the past century, Nietzsche and Freud, and one of the most influential modern poets, Rainer Maria Rilke. These and other less famous but formidable intellects, lovers and friends, all seem to have been completely bewitched by Lou Andreas-Salome. One need only read a passage from her memoirs or any of her twenty books or other writings to discover in her what could bring a giant to his knees. She possessed a radiance of spirit and a keenness of mind that inspires worship. I am certain the source of her luster was her heartfelt "reverence for a deeply shared destiny with all things." Lou Andreas-Salome's novels, her correspondence with Rilke, and her works on Freud and Nietzsche are in English translation. Her memoirs, *Looking Back,* are not to be missed.

Hannah Arendt (1906–1975)

GERMAN-BORN AMERICAN POLITICAL SCIENTIST
AND PHILOSOPHER

Hannah Arendt was established as a major political thinker by her monumental work, *Origins of Totalitarianism,* and her critical writings on Jewish affairs. A fugitive from the Nazis, known for her potent intellectual confrontation of anti-Semitism, Arendt had an abstruse lifelong relationship with philosopher Martin Heideger, a Nazi sympathizer. Scholars emphasize that understanding the mutual dependence and influence of this profound, enigmatic relationship is key to understanding either of these powerful intellectual figures. Hannah Arendt became a U.S. citizen in 1951; she lectured at major universities, served on the faculty of the University of Chicago and the New York School for Social Research, and held leadership roles with the Conference on Jewish Relations and with Jewish Cultural Reconstruction, Inc., which sought to salvage Jewish writings dispersed by the Nazis. Among her many excellent works, her *Essays in Understanding* and *The Life of the Mind* are outstanding.

Aung San Suu Kyi (born 1945)

BURMESE HUMAN-RIGHTS ACTIVIST

Aung San Suu Kyi's father, U Aung San, national hero of independent Burma, was assassinated when she was two years old. She attended school in Burma, in India when her diplomat mother was ambassador there, and finally at the University of Oxford where she met her future husband and the father of her two children. In 1988 she returned to Burma to care for her dying mother, a trip from which she did not return. The oppression of the Burmese by the Ne Win military and the erupting revolution catapulted Aung San Suu Kyi into a role she embraced as her destiny and as the legacy of her father. She organized nonviolent protests and a campaign for democracy and human rights. She became the central figure in the National League for Democracy which won eighty-two percent of the parliamentary seats in the 1990 election but was never permitted to take power. Placed under house arrest and held incommunicado, she was told she could leave the country quietly and be with her family but refused to do so until civilian government was restored and political prisoners were released. In 1991 when she was awarded the Nobel Peace Prize, her husband, Michael Aris, did not know whether she was even alive, let alone whether she was aware of having won the prestigious prize. Her son, Alexander Aris, accepted the Nobel on her behalf. Aung San Suu Kyi has given us a glimpse of the ultimate heights of our humanity. She remains a symbol of courage and freedom for people in Burma and throughout the world. Her eloquent voice for *Freedom from Fear* is heard through her essays, assembled by her husband and with a forward by Vaclav Havel.

Jane Austen (1775–1817)

ENGLISH NOVELIST

We will find no more authentic portrait of middle-class provincial life in eighteenth-century England than through the piercing perception of Jane Austen. The daughter of a Hampshire rector and one of eight children, Jane Austen began writing at an early age for the "theatre," which was the family's amusement. She never married and rarely traveled; the limited scope of her everyday life became the vast arena of her boundless imaginings. Her delightfully detailed depiction of family relations and of extraordinary love in ordinary life gave her novels their enduring quality. Today's renaissance of her novels through film—most notably Emma Thompson's *Sense and Sensibility*, Andrew Davies' *Pride and Prejudice* and Nick Dear's

Persuasion—affirms their timelessness. Her most glowing presence remains in the written word, straight from her hand to the enamored readers who have elevated her to the illustriousness she so thoroughly deserves.

Simone de Beauvoir (1908–1986)

FRENCH PHILOSOPHER AND AUTHOR

One of the grande dames of French intellectual life, Simone de Beauvoir is best known for *Le Deuxieme Sexe (The Second Sex)*. This classic of feminist literature, translated into twenty-six languages, is as provocative today as it was during its popularity in the 1960s. Simone de Beauvoir was a lifelong companion of Jean-Paul Sartre and a partner in and proponent of his Existentialist philosophy. She taught philosophy in France, lectured in the U.S. on contemporary French literature, was a prolific writer and an impassioned activist for women's rights and for egalitarian relations between men and women. Though she railed against the myth of a specifically female nature as conceived, or imposed, by patriarchal ideology, she also said she was surprised to discover that the first thing she had to say about herself was "I am a woman."

Charlotte Brontë (1816–1855)

ENGLISH NOVELIST

For many young women, *Jane Eyre* was among their first great reading experiences. When its publisher stepped out of a meeting in 1848 and barked, "Well, young woman, what do you want of me?" he was stunned to discover that the fragile female who stood before him was the author of *Jane Eyre*; Charlotte had published it under a male pseudonym. The third of six children of a Yorkshire minister, Charlotte was the strongest character in her family as well as in her novels, which were more the product of ingeniously detailed documentation than imagination. Her two elder sisters died and she herself became ill due to the treatment endured in a boarding school like the one depicted in *Jane Eyre*. Her vivid expression of the female heart exhibited in all of her novels was the result of a shattering love affair from which she never completely recovered. Though she did enjoy renown as an author during her lifetime, it seems a paltry recompense for the hardship she endured. Her mother died when she was five and her weak father was as much burden as he was support; she lost her three remaining younger siblings, including her most beloved sister, Emily, all in one year, and her earnest efforts to support her family with her writing were assailed as an immoral, unwomanly invasion of a rightfully male profession. She is now regarded as one of the greatest female novelists of the nineteenth century.

Emily Brontë (1818–1848)

ENGLISH POET AND NOVELIST

Where her sister Charlotte possessed a bold heroic character, Emily's was less visible, except to her sister. Charlotte recognized in Emily's enigmatic nature the purity of her individuality and the great power of her intellect. Charlotte and Emily were extremely close, and though they expressed themselves differently, they shared admirable traits which they both possessed in remarkable measure. When Emily was bitten by a mad dog, she burned her wound with a hot iron and did not speak a word of the incident to the family until she was out of danger. She was equally reserved about her profound artistic gifts. She would never have shared her poetry with her family, much less published it, were it not for Charlotte's discovery and persistent urgings. Emily's only novel, the dark romantic tragedy *Wuthering Heights,* depicts the wild Yorkshire moors of the Brontë home where Emily spent most of her life until she died at age thirty. Although her novel is a literary masterpiece, her true passion was her poetry. Of the three sisters who wrote, Charlotte, Emily, and Ann, Emily is now recognized as the one possessing true poetic genius.

Elizabeth Barrett Browning (1806–1861)

ENGLISH POET

From a very early age, Elizabeth Barrett was passionate about reading and writing. She was of fragile health most of her life, which kept her at home for her schooling. For the eldest of eleven siblings, desperate to read, convalescence may have been the only available instrument for her purpose! She devoured literature and history and metaphysics, learned six languages, and translated Greek and Byzantine verse without ever going to school. With the same fervor, while still very young, she devoted herself to the poetry that would later establish her as a major literary figure. As a young woman, her romantic verse touched the heart of another poet and inspired a classic love correspondence and literary union. She and Robert Browning secretly wed and moved away from Elizabeth's despotic father who had forbidden his children to marry. She lived happily in Florence with her husband and her son and enjoyed a social circle which included Ruskin, Tennyson, Hawthorne, Thackeray, and Carlyle.

Willa Cather (1873–1947)

AMERICAN NOVELIST

Willa Cather grew up amidst frontier life on the great plains of Red Cloud, Nebraska. Her portrayal of European immigrants breaking the land and building a life on the American prairie would stake her claim on the landscape of American literature. As a student at the University of Nebraska, she demonstrated a marked talent for journalism. After graduating she took a position with a Pittsburgh magazine and then went on to be copy editor and music and drama editor of the *Pittsburgh Leader.* She published short stories, taught writing, worked as editor of another magazine, until at the age of thirty-five she left her job to devote herself entirely to her novels. It was then, under the influence of Sarah Orne Jewett's "regionalism," that she turned to what she knew best—the wide-open spaces of the American frontier. Her deep spiritual attachment to the Nebraska of her youth yielded the masterworks *My Antonia, O Pioneers!, A Lost Lady,* and her Pulitzer Prize winning *One of Ours.*

Colette (1873–1954)

FRENCH AUTHOR

One of France's most cherished female authors, Sidonie Gabrielle Colette produced more than seventy works—novels, plays, film scripts, short stories, and reviews. She is best known to Americans for *Gigi* (1943) which was adapted for both stage and screen. Collette celebrated the vibrance of life in all she wrote. From her teenage years in the dance halls of Paris to her unguarded treatment of aging in her final writings, she possessed an honesty and an effervescence that endeared her to generations. She was sensuous and sensitive and acutely observant of nature; she said her wise mother had awakened her to the wonders of "everything that germinates, blossoms, or flies." She wrote about love and life as it was—laced throughout with evocative cadences of indulgent pleasure. At times she was scandalous—to American readers, anyway. To the French she was the marvelous Colette, member of the Belgian Royal Academy, the French Academie Goncourt, and a grand officer of the Legion d'Honneur—honors rarely granted to women.

Marie Curie (1867–1934)

POLISH-BORN FRENCH PHYSICIST

Albert Einstein spoke of Marie Curie as the only celebrated being whom fame had not corrupted. The first woman to win the Nobel Prize for Physics, the first person to win two Nobel Prizes, Marie Curie's contribution to science was inestimable.

But beneath the public persona—the formidable physicist and chemist, the Nobel laureate, the first female professor at the Sorbonne—we find a remarkable woman. As a teenager in Poland she worked to help support her family and volunteered time reading to women workers. As a young woman she used her governess earnings to put her sister through medical school. Her example as a mother both encouraged and inspired; her daughter also became a Nobel laureate. And after the sudden death of the man who was both her husband and her partner in science, she carried on their work until she died of the leukemia resulting from her exposure to radioactive substances. Marie Curie was among those rare beings who wield celebrity with a deep sense of global responsibility. Her words to the United Nations reflect her profound contribution to humanity.

Bernadette Devlin McAliskey (born 1947)

NORTHERN IRISH CIVIL RIGHTS ACTIVIST

In 1969 Alvin Shuster in *The New York Times Book Review* wrote that much of the credit for waking up London and the world to the trouble brewing in Northern Ireland must go to Bernadette Devlin. Bernadette's father's bedtime stories were not of fairies and princesses but of Irish history filtered through the lens of the struggling working class. After her father's death, her family subsisted on welfare; Bernadette managed to put herself through college. In 1968 during a civil rights demonstration she watched the police beat a young man who tried to protect her. From that day forward, she was a one-woman tempest of activism for the working class of Ireland, a commitment that did not falter in the face of repeated arrests, months in prison, and bullet wounds sustained by her and by her husband, Michael McAliskey. She campaigned tirelessly and became the youngest woman ever elected to the British Parliament where she was its most vocal and controversial member. Her autobiography, *The Price of My Soul,* has been described as a "monument to the struggle of the powerless against the powerful."

Emily Dickinson (1830–1886)

AMERICAN POET

During her lifetime, only seven of Emily Dickinson's poems were published—and those were heavily edited and without attribution. Today her 1,775 poems together with her artful correspondence comprise one of the great literary treasures. The second of three children, and granddaughter of one of the founders of Amherst College, Emily was educated at Amherst, never married, and spent most of her life within the boundary of her family's property. A voracious reader, she consumed the works of Ralph Waldo Emerson, she adored George Sand and Jane Austen and all the great women writers before her, she committed to memory every lyrical syllable of the poetry of Elizabeth Barrett Browning for whom she possessed an unrivaled devotion. What emerged from Emily Dickinson's isolation with great literature was the passionate, witty, transcendent poetry of the "belle of Amherst."

Annie Dillard (born 1945)

AMERICAN AUTHOR

A few years ago I had the privilege of hearing Annie Dillard speak at a university, something she rarely does. I came away from the relaxed reading and question-and-answer presentation feeling I had just encountered one of the most brilliant minds on the planet. I was particularly struck by her response to a student, "I am not a feminist writer. I am a writer and I am a woman." I have continued to be amazed by Annie Dillard—the sheer elegance of the crafting of *An American Childhood* and *Pilgrim at Tinker Creek* (which won the Pulitzer Prize), the raw intelligence of *Living by Fiction,* the depth and breadth of *The Living.* There are great writers and there are individuals who when they speak cannot avoid saying something of import. Annie Dillard is both. Her other great works include *Teaching a Stone to Talk* and *The Writing Life.*

H. D. (Hilda Doolittle, 1886–1961)

AMERICAN POET

"H.D."'s *Collected Poems 1912–1944* secured her position as a major twentieth-century poet. She won additional acclaim for her translations of Greek dramas and for her prose. The daughter of an astronomer at the University of Pennsylvania and reared in the strict Moravian tradition of her mother's family, Hilda Doolittle moved to Europe in her mid-twenties and lived there for the rest of her life. Her poetry was influenced by Ezra Pound, to whom she was briefly engaged, and by her husband, Richard Aldington. Throughout her life she was encircled by literary friends, including D. H. Lawrence, Marianne Moore, T. S. Eliot, Amy Lowell, and William Carlos Williams. Her autobiographical works include *Bid Me to Live, Tribute to Freud,* and *End to Torment.*

Isadora Duncan (1877–1927)

AMERICAN DANCER AND
AN ORIGINATOR OF INTERPRETIVE DANCE

Isadora Duncan lived her life the same way she danced—in her bare feet, in flamboyant defiance of anything artificial or restrictive. Her life was both a grand drama and a heart-breaking tragedy. Raised in San Francisco by her music teacher mother, she rejected the rigid constriction of classic ballet. At twenty-one, feeling that the artistry of her natural interpretive dance was misunderstood in the U.S., she determined to find recognition abroad. With her meager savings, she sailed on a cattle boat to England where she began her love-hate relationship with another continent. Dancing throughout Europe, she was at times a sensation, but Isadora paid a high price for her fidelity to her genius and to the revolutionary spirit that ruled her. She suffered condemnation throughout her scandalous life, she lost both of her beloved illegitimate children in a tragic accident, her abusive husband committed suicide, her schools failed, and her desperate need for recognition was never satiated. She died as she lived and as she danced—her long dramatic scarf became entangled in the rear wheel of the car in which she was riding and she was strangled. Isadora Duncan is credited with paving the way for modern dance.

Isabelle Eberhardt (1877–1904)

SWISS-BORN, RUSSIAN-EDUCATED
NORTH AFRICAN WANDERER

It is difficult to imagine a more turbulent journey through life than that traveled by Isabelle Eberhardt. She was born near Geneva, the illegitimate daughter of a Russian revolutionary. Her mother took Isabelle when she was a child and left her husband to be with Isabelle's father, a tyrant whose only merit as a parent was his knowledge of languages—Isabelle learned seven. When she was twenty, she and her mother fled another marriage, this time to North Africa where they converted to the Muslim faith. Soon after, her mother died and Isabelle wandered aimlessly in the desert; she donned male attire, took numerous lovers, was ravaged by starvation, disease, and excessive alcohol. She died at twenty-eight in a flash flood near the Algerian-Moroccan border. Among her few possessions were her journals, published in *Dans l'Ombre Chaude d'Islam* and *Pages d'Islam.* More of her writings were discovered later and published under the fitting title of one of her essays, *The Oblivion Seekers.* Writing was for Isabelle Eberhardt a solitary refuge from a wretched existence. Her words reflect a radiant nobility of spirit and a striking depth of soul.

George Eliot (Marian Evans, 1819–1880)

ENGLISH NOVELIST

The incomparable English novelist George Eliot was an insatiable reader as a child and an exemplary student of languages, literature, and philosophy. She eagerly embraced the religious fervor instilled during her youth until in her early twenties, much to the consternation of her religious father, she broke from orthodoxy and became a free thinker. Her keen mind gravitated toward the study of the relationship between religion and science and the doubts they were both designed to dispel. She worked as an editor for *The Westminster Review*, wrote essays, translated Spinoza, had friendly correspondence with American author Harriet Beecher Stowe and Russian writer Ivan Turgenev, and continued her study of philosophy. The opportunity to devote herself entirely to her novels came hand-in-hand with the most significant relationship of her life. George Henry Lewes was a writer-philosopher, a Goethe scholar, and an ardent admirer of George Sand (another "George"—Marian Evans' pseudonym demonstrates high regard for the name), Jane Austen, Charlotte Brontë, and other great female writers. George Eliot lived with Lewes until his death. He took great joy in the recognition and support of George Eliot's genius, the genius that would produce *Middlemarch, Silas Marner, Adam Bede, The Mill on the Floss,* and *Daniel Deronda.*

Margaret Fuller (1810–1850)

AMERICAN CRITIC AND AUTHOR

"Such a predetermination to eat this big universe as her oyster or egg I have not before seen in any human soul," wrote English essayist and historian Thomas Carlyle of Margaret Fuller, who stirred the same measure of response in Emerson, Thoreau, Hawthorne, and Henry James. Elizabeth Barrett Browning said, "Her writings were curiously inferior to her conversation." A child prodigy who read Virgil, Ovid, and Horace at the age of seven, Margaret Fuller was tireless in her intellectual pursuits as well as in her crusade for equality for women. She was the first self-supporting female American journalist and foreign correspondent. Her critical essays won her the positions of editor of the Transcendentalist quarterly *The Dial* and literary critic for the *New York Tribune.* A champion of George Sand and an accomplished interpreter of modern European literature, she wrote her most cherished and expansive work on Goethe, and her 1846 *Papers on Literature and Art* brought her genuine literary distinction. She was a charismatic organizer and facilitator of what are known today as "women's groups," and her masterwork, *Woman in the Nineteenth Century* (1845), is a classic of feminist literature. Margaret Fuller died at the age of forty when she and her husband and their infant son perished in a shipwreck off Fire Island. Though subsequent biographers trivialized this woman of letters, she was a significant force in the history of American culture.

Gildas

(A SPIRIT WHO CHANNELS THROUGH RUTH WHITE)

While visiting England, in an elegant bed-and-breakfast Knightsbridge home, I enjoyed wonderful conversation with my host, a woman of uncommon dignity and spirit, a psychologist and writer. When I awoke one morning, on my nightstand lay an unassuming little pamphlet of a book with a striking title: *Sexuality & Spirituality,* "by Gildas, channeled through Ruth White." My host knew I would find it intriguing. Perceiving significance in every serendipitous contact with extraordinary women and their words, I was receptive. As it turned out, words in that little book became integral to *The Words of a Woman.* The wisdom from the spirit, Gildas, also concretized my own intuitive notions about the profound relationship between two essential aspects of our being, one being an expression of the other. Do I believe that spirits channel through human beings? If the mystery of life has taught me anything, it has taught me to disbelieve nothing.

Joan Halifax (born 1942)

AMERICAN ANTHROPOLOGIST, ECOLOGIST, AND AUTHOR

While casting the net for extraordinary women living today who have expressed themselves in writing, I contacted the Institute for Noetic Sciences, an international organization that focuses on the mind's diverse ways of knowing and encourages dialogue among leading-edge thinkers. The first name that surfaced was Joan Halifax. A Buddhist, anthropologist, ecologist, and author,

Joan Halifax has worked over the years as a scientist, scholar, and educator with diverse institutions including the National Science Foundation, the New School for Social Research, Esalen Institute, the Association of Humanistic Psychology, and numerous universities. She has been a pioneer in the synergism of Eastern thought with Western science, has collaborated with Joseph Campbell on his *Historical Atlas of World Mythology*, and co-authored *The Human Encounter* with Stanislav Grof. She currently heads a nonprofit Buddhist organization in Santa Fe, New Mexico, called Upaya (Sanskrit word for "the craft of compassion"), which is grounded in the belief that all things are interconnected and that the well-being of others is intimately related to our own. Much of her work has been devoted to compassionate care for the dying. Among Joan Halifax's written works are *The Fruitful Darkness, The Journey of Initiation*, and *Shamanic Voices: A Survey of Visionary Narratives.*

Alice James (1848–1892)

AMERICAN SOUL-SEARCHER
(AND SISTER OF HENRY AND WILLIAM)

Virginia Woolf's Shakespeare's sister would certainly have found a kindred spirit in the woman who was the sister of both Henry James and William James! As Henry put it, "In our family, girls seem scarcely to have had a chance." (Alice was the only female of five children.) A mid-nineteenth-century New Yorker, overshadowed by the mighty males in her household, Alice James was not lacking in the full depth of character, intellect, and soul with which her famous brothers were endowed. She also possessed a gift for expression. Were she not the sister of one of the greatest American novelists and a preeminent psychologist/philosopher, her diaries and letters would likely never have found their way into print and Alice James' resplendence would have remained unrevealed. In her voice we hear what may well have been the expression of Shakespeare's sister: "When I am gone, pray don't think of me as a creature who might have been something else. Notwithstanding the poverty of my outside experience, I have always had a significance for myself, and every chance to stumble along my straight and narrow little path, and to worship at the feet of my Deity, and for what more can a human soul ask?"

Sarah Orne Jewett (1849–1909)

AMERICAN AUTHOR

To classify *The Country of the Pointed Firs* as "regionalism" or as anything but awe-inspiring strikes me as being much like stuffing a peacock into a bureau drawer. Sarah Orne Jewett's incomparable work about the coastal Maine village in which she lived underscored, for her protégé Willa Cather and for all writers, the importance of writing about the thing we know best. Jewett possessed a transcendent mastery of language, a relationship *with* language. The daughter of a country doctor, she was determined to write about the rapidly disappearing traditions of provincial life around her. She sold her first story when she was eighteen and continued to write "local color" pieces which were published by *The Atlantic, Harper's,* and *The Century.* By the age of twenty-eight she was an established writer.

Her father, with whom she shared intelligent companionship, was the central figure in her life. She never married but had great bonds of friendship with women. She loved her home and her surroundings, and most of all, her writing. Her finest work is also represented in *Deephaven*.

Doris Lessing (born 1919)

BRITISH AUTHOR

One of the most brilliant voices of modern literature, Doris Lessing has never hesitated to take on the world on her own terms. Her political activist roots run deep into her childhood in Rhodesia (now Zimbabwe), where she observed the racial strife of British colonial Africa. Through half a century, her work has evolved from her early *African Stories* to novels, short stories, and essays which have been the medium for her treatment of aging, child-rearing, education, madness, politics, male-female relations, and every issue relevant to humanity. Her science fiction of recent years is dazzling. *The Golden Notebook* and *A Small Personal Voice* instill in a writer the hope of some measure of osmosis—an infusion of her brilliance, her courage, her candor. Doris Lessing is more than a master of the craft, she is a force to be reckoned with. Her sheer personal power will project her voice for centuries as one of the wisest of our time. Her other great works include *The Memoirs of a Survivor, A Man and Two Women, The Sun Between Their Feet,* and *The Marriage Between Zones Three, Four and Five.*

Anne Morrow Lindbergh (born 1906)

AMERICAN AVIATOR AND AUTHOR

For millions of women, Anne Morrow Lindbergh is remembered most, not as the wife of the world-famous aviator who braved the Atlantic, nor for the Lindberghs' tragic lunge back into the limelight by the kidnap-murder of their two-year-old son. Rather, Anne Morrow Lindbergh is remembered by many as the author of a little book that came to them as a gift from a sister, a mother, a friend—a book they have given in turn to another, a daughter, a confidante. *Gift from the Sea* is just that—a gift of pearls from the sea of experience, reflections on life and relationship, as simple as a sea pebble, as comforting and as fortifying as the sound of the sea. "Perhaps both men and women in America hunger, in our material . . . active, masculine culture, for the supposedly feminine qualities of heart, mind and spirit—qualities which are actually neither masculine nor feminine, but simply human qualities that have been neglected . . . It may be our special function to emphasize again these neglected realities . . . as a first real step toward a deeper understanding . . . they are the essence of life itself."

Katherine Mansfield (1888–1923)

NEW ZEALAND–BORN ENGLISH AUTHOR

The impression left upon me by Katherine Mansfield personalizes the sensory experience of literature which I feel is literature's highest purpose. We are left with a profound feeling that the author's soul has somehow fused with our own. Her husband, critic, essayist, and editor John Middleton Murry, came as close as I can imagine to describing the soul and style that is uniquely Katherine Mansfield: "I can only describe it as a kind of purity . . . natural and spontaneous as was no other human being I have ever met. She adjusted herself to life as a flower adjusts itself to the earth and to the sun. She suffered greatly, she delighted greatly, but her suffering and her delight were never partial, they filled the whole of her. When she gave herself—to life, to love, to some spirit of truth which she served—she gave royally . . . this preoccupation with truth, in what she told and in herself to be worthy to tell it, became her devouring passion." Katherine Mansfield's beautiful stories are collected in *The Garden Party, Bliss and Other Stories,* and *The Stories of Katherine Mansfield.*

Beryl Markham (1902–1986)

BRITISH EAST AFRICAN AVIATOR AND
FIRST SOLO PILOT TO CROSS ATLANTIC TO THE WEST

Beryl Markham spent most of her life in Kenya where as a young woman she became the first female to obtain a commercial pilot's license. Her career as a bush pilot took her into remote regions of Africa where she would land in forest clearings and fields to deliver mail, passengers, and supplies. For pure adventure she undertook a number of daring solo flights; and in spite of the mid-flight failed engines, force-downs by storms, and blustering desert gale maroonings, she still had her eye on the prize. Charles Lindbergh had made it *from* the west, but no one had faced the prevailing winds and crossed the

Atlantic *to* the west; she was determined to fly from London to New York. Though her plane crash-landed in Nova Scotia, Markham survived the trip to world astonishment and acclaim. Her poetic 1942 autobiography, *West with the Night,* was revived in 1983 to become a best-seller. Whether it was written exclusively by her hand or, as recently alleged, by her third husband, a writer, it was at the very least a collaboration and a vivid portrayal of an extraordinary woman's life.

Gabriela Mistral (1889–1957)

CHILEAN POET

The first Latin American woman to win the Nobel Prize for Literature (1945), Lucila Godoy Alcayago chose a pen name that honored two of her favorite poets, Gabriele D'Annanzio and Frederic Mistral. She grew up in a village in northern Chile, became a schoolteacher at fifteen, and was an established poet by her mid-twenties. She wrote verse throughout her life and her career as a college professor, cultural minister, and diplomat. An ambassadorship afforded her extensive travel, and her diplomatic assignments took her to Madrid, Lisbon, Genoa, and Nice. She served on sociological and cultural committees of the League of Nations and the United Nations. She never married and never recovered from a young love that ended in the tragic suicide of her lover after their breakup. Her emotional poetry expresses the heart of a woman deeply affected by love and maternal longings. Collections of her poems have been translated widely, including *The Selected Poems of Gabriela Mistral* by Doris Dana.

Marlo Morgan

AMERICAN EXPLORER AND SOUL-SEARCHER

Marlo Morgan's *Mutant Message Down Under* was handed to me by a dear friend while I was vacationing in Colorado. It fit perfectly with the spirit of relaxation and adventure—a simply written story about a woman's awakening to what really matters in life through a walkabout with an Aboriginal tribe. I have since read some of the criticism about her writing, her exploitation of the Aborigines, her earnings from the book. Though I have gained some sense of her harshest critics, their words offer little enlightenment about who Marlo Morgan is. I know that she wrote about an extraordinary experience convincingly enough to reach the multitude who have found her best-selling book worth reading and passing along. I know that the simple truths she extolled were consistent with the ideas of some extraordinary people and worthy of rediscovery in a new and creative form. I know that I could not resist including her particular words in *The Words of a Woman*. And I know for certain that the wisdom and fortitude that comes from the kind of experience she described, whether real-life or fiction, will be well served in the current walkabout—the controversy about whether her story is true and whether she had the right to tell it. Haven't we all gained strength of character from both real life and fiction.

Florence Nightingale (1820–1910)

ENGLISH NURSE AND FOUNDER
OF PROFESSIONAL NURSING FOR WOMEN

"Lady of the Lamp" Florence Nightingale lived in England at a time when females of her class were expected to oversee their children's moral training, grace their husband's tables, and dress to please. Her proposal to study nursing was refused. She took her nursing training in Germany and gained an appointment as superintendent of a London nursing facility. The Crimean War thrust her into increasingly responsible roles in the care of wounded British soldiers. Within a year she was general superintendent of Female Nursing for the Military Hospitals of the Army, an appointment she was not awarded officially until a year later. Deplorable hospital conditions and the welfare of the soldiers became her burning concern, and she used her popularity with the British people to influence the queen; a Royal Commission was established to oversee improvements. With funds she received from the public she established the Nightingale School for Nurses, the first of its kind in the world, creating a new and respectable profession for women when females of any class had few ways to earn a decent livelihood. She went on to initiate training for midwives and for nurses in poorhouse infirmaries. She influenced significant health reforms. And throughout, Florence Nightingale remained "brutally indifferent to whether a woman ought or ought not to have done what I have done." Three years before her death, she became the first woman to be awarded the Order of Merit by the King of England.

Flannery O'Connor (1925–1964)

AMERICAN AUTHOR

Flannery O'Connor in her later years would be one of the crispest, most colorful characters a storyteller could ever hope to capture—settled on her family's ancestral Georgian farm, she and her mother doting on ducks and geese and peafowl strutting around the barnyard; sneering defiantly at the lupus that crippled her for the last decade of her life; spinning yarns with the local folk, and writing her stories. And as with any vibrant character in a great novel, we discover in the simplest life a complexity of nature that holds our attention long after their story is told. Flannery O'Connor was as intense a mystic-metaphysician as Simone Weil, and she effortlessly hurled the kind of playful cerebral daggers that could have had Dorothy Parker in stitches. A devout Catholic all her life, she challenged the Church for its every weakness as she challenged any weakness of devotion to the Church. She told what she knew through what she knew best—real life in the rural South. But her works defy categorization. She surely perfected her craft under the superb tutelage of the University of Iowa's writing program, but originality is not something we learn. Flannery O'Connor was an original. *Wise Blood* and *Everything That Rises Must Converge* and all of her stories are great. Her collected letters, *The Habit of Being,* is a rare find.

Katherine Anne Porter (1890–1980)

AMERICAN AUTHOR

Known for her mastery of short fiction and her novel *Ship of Fools*, Katherine Anne Porter earned both the Pulitzer Prize and the National Book Award for her *Collected Stories*. A rural Texan coeval with the bulk of the twentieth century, she said she spent all of her intellectual and spiritual energy trying to grasp both the grandeur and the great failure of humanity in the Western world. Having been in Mexico during the retrenchment after the Revolution, in Germany when the Nazis were siezing power, and in Washington, D.C., during World War II and the Kennedy and Johnson administrations, she once told Flannery O'Connor she wished she knew who exactly was in charge of this universe. Her own words best express her literary legacy: "The voice of an individual artist may seem perhaps of no more consequence than the whirring of a cricket in the grass; but the arts do live continuously . . . they live literally by faith . . . through times of interruption, diminishment, and neglect; they outlive governments and creeds and societies, even the very civilizations that produced them . . . They represent the substance of faith . . . and even the smallest and most incomplete offering . . . can be a proud act in defense of that faith."

Ayn Rand (1905–1982)

RUSSIAN-BORN AMERICAN PHILOSOPHER AND AUTHOR

Ayn Rand will always be inextricably linked in my mind with the one classroom teacher who taught me to think. Jackie Plas was a "Randite." I also believe it was *Atlas Shrugged* that first gave form to some of my earliest instincts about myself. The popular novel had a similar effect on a number of significant females in my life. Her philosophical work—the austere, relentless Objectivism that is uniquely Rand—has served me best as a catalyst, a fierce blow from the far edge which pushes the pendulum back and puts deliberate conscious force into its motion. Ayn Rand was a deep intellectual with an iron grip on her own individuality. As ferocious as she was about her fundamental truths, there was enough of her to be a hopeful romantic as well; her quintessential heroes, Dagny Taggart and John Galt, remain with one for a lifetime. Ayn Rand's other absorbing novel, *The Fountainhead*, stands out from her Objectivist works, *The Virtue of Selfishness, The Objectivist, The Ayn Rand Letter,* and *For the New Intellectual.*

George Sand
(Amantine Aurore Lucile Dupin, 1804–1876)

FRENCH ROMANTIC AUTHOR

Amantine Aurore Lucile Dupin was the physical manifestation of a volcanic soul and an incandescent spirit. More than a woman who made herself over into a man to be taken seriously as a writer, she was everything to which a male or female writer could aspire. The great authors whose ink has flowed under her influence are innumerable. Henry James called her "the great magician," and the greatest magician of all, Marcel Proust, adored her throughout his life. Popular culture has portrayed her as a fiery, independent, promiscuous femme who cast aside her husband for a thrilling bohemian life. A more ludicrous misconception of a woman who had not a casual cell in her being is not to be imagined. Her rare moral character needed no instruction; its roots were cemented in the depth of her being. She left her husband because he was dark and brutal. Her lovers were younger because she objected to intimacies with married men. She took love, whether romance or friendship, where she could revel in the authenticity of both the person and the feeling; she could only have wished for as many opportunities as were alleged. Though it could not be admitted publicly in a culture that wanted its great heroes to be great men, George Sand was the most widely read and respected author among the intelligentsia of her century, and her unparalleled influence has touched every writer since. How could such luminesence remain but a spark in the mainstream? I wonder, had "Aurore" truly been a "George."

POET OF ANCIENT GREECE

Imagine how a poet of seventh-century B.C.E. would feel to see her words traveling as "poetry in motion" on a public-transit-system bus at the end of the twentieth century. The resurgence of interest in this mythic character, the great lyric poet of ancient Greece, enlivens the temporal with a touch of antiquity and a sparkle of romance. For a time, both Sappho and her poetry were virtually eliminated from history. What we know about her has been pieced together from papyrus fragments unearthed around 1900 and from references to her in ancient Greek literature. Some scholars say her work was considered obscene by the church and was destroyed. She is alleged to have been the founder of a school for women that had music at the core of its curriculum and that taught young women about love and the perfection of womanhood. She is known to have sung her poetry accompanied by the melodic strains from the twenty-one-string lyre she played. Of her nine books of poems and songs, only a few hundred lines of poetry and fragments have been recovered. Her Sapphic stanza remains influential with poets today, and her timeless lyric verse continues to captivate.

May Sarton (1912–1995)

BELGIAN-BORN AMERICAN POET AND NOVELIST

"In whatever May Sarton writes one can hear the human heart pulsing just below the surface." "This artist reveals herself fully, and outlines the spirit of the times as well." The daughter of an eminent Harvard history of science professor and an artist mother, Eleanore Marie Sarton began writing poetry and keeping a journal when she was a young girl. As a young woman she was active in repertory theatre, producing, directing, and acting. She taught creative writing in Boston and English composition at Harvard; later she read her poetry and lectured throughout the United States. Her body of work, a staggering twenty novels and twenty-five volumes of poetry and memoirs, enjoys increasing recognition. She "holds herself up for all to see," said one critic of this writer who has lived up to her conviction that "the deeper you go into the personal—the more you hit the universal."

Olive Schreiner (1855–1920)

SOUTH AFRICAN AUTHOR

How could a major literary and social-political force in her lifetime—her famous novel hailed as one of the finest in the English language—have fallen into virtual obscurity? Doris Lessing, who shares Olive Schreiner's African roots, explains that both Olive Schreiner and her enormous influence are hidden within the events she helped to shape. Her novel, *The Story of an African Farm,* involved people around the world in absorbing real-life relationships set in Africa—for most a faraway land of wild animals and savage uprisings. As a famous author she was an audible voice for the African people. Her appeal for the poor and for oppressed women, *Women and Labour* became a bible of the feminist movement. Olive Schreiner had no formal education; her intuitive intelligence took her deep into Goethe, Montaigne, Carlyle, Locke, J. S. Mill, Shakespeare, Darwin, Ruskin, and Schiller while in her teens. As an adolescent she began a complex, lifelong struggle with spirituality, finally reconciling in a deeply held belief in the universe as a living oneness that is *nothing but* God. Above all, Olive Schreiner remained faithful to her own organic nature and to the kind of raw exposure that drives truth out of every pore. She is remembered by Doris Lessing and other admirers as a writer whose greatness lies very simply in the indelibility of the feeling her writing inspires.

Mary Shelley (1799–1851)

ENGLISH AUTHOR

The bright and accomplished daughter of notable intellectual radicals, pioneer feminist Mary Wollstonecraft and political philosopher William Goodwin, Mary Shelley had the kind of childhood unique to progeny of gifted and famous parents. She would hide behind the sofa in the late evening and listen to recitations by the great writers who regularly visited her parents' home. At sixteen she eloped with one of those gifted friends of her father, poet Percy Bysshe Shelley, for whom she was the consummate partner in their shared world of poetry and philosophy. When she was just nineteen she wrote the novel that would become the most famous horror story of all time. The idea came to her one rainy London evening when she and Shelley and Lord Byron passed the time telling ghost stories and decided they would each create one. Her harrowing fantasy about a scientist's perilous tampering with the creation of life takes on even more tragic tones when we learn how Mary Shelley was relentlessly stalked by death throughout her life. Her mother died shortly after giving her birth; she herself suffered numerous miscarriages, one that almost killed her; two of her surviving children died very young; other family members committed suicide, and her beloved husband was lost at sea at the age of thirty. Her most famous creation, whose name evokes the image of the world's most popular monster, *Frankenstein* is a novel that reads like a great tragic melody.

Gertrude Stein (1874–1946)

AMERICAN AUTHOR

In an orchestra of literary women, Virginia Woolf would be asked to conduct—surely one of George Sand's compositions. Jane Austen would play first violin and Jeanne de Vietinghoff the harp. There is one other position that is at once crystal clear in my mind: Gertrude Stein on tuba. But only if the arrangement called for only one. One bold booming tuba. Thundering blasts and recurring reverberations. Anyone who knows Gertrude Stein understands this image. Her greatest pleasure in life, perhaps her mission, was to stand out. And that she did. Her writing was a literary revolution. After studying psychology with William James at Radcliffe, and medicine at Johns Hopkins, she took up residence in Paris where for years her famous salon featured Picasso, Renoir, and Matisse on the walls and Picasso, Hemingway, and Alfred North Whitehead as her regular visitors. With language, she was both musician and magician—she exploited and embellished its inherent qualities of sound. And like her friend Picasso, she broke all the rules. Some found her treatment of language to be frivolous and abusive and uncouth; others believed her genius was just too enormous to be contained within existing forms. She never responded to either with anything but her own truth: "if you have vitality enough of knowing enough of what you mean, somebody and sometimes a great many will have to realize that you know what you mean and so they will agree that you mean what you know, which is as near as anybody can come to understanding any one."

Ting Ling (Chiang Wei-Chih, 1904–1986)

CHINESE AUTHOR

One of the most important female writers of twentieth-century China, Ting Ling expresses a distinctly female perspective on life, love, and the revolutionary struggles of a gender and a people. Born in the Hunan province, she was educated in provincial schools and then traveled to Shanghai, Nanking, and Peking where her intellectual pursuits combined with her partnership with a leftist poet induced an increasingly turbulent involvement in politics. Her husband was executed by Nationalist authorities and she was later imprisoned for five years during the Cultural Revolution. Though her proletarian works were acclaimed, she openly criticized the party, particularly concerning women's rights. Her essays, short stories, and longer fictional prose are studied widely as the works of a fascinating, independent, and emotionally complex Chinese woman, not unlike the passionate characters portrayed in her stories of unrequited love and the bewildering search for the meaning of life. Her writing possesses something more than the influence of Flaubert and other European greats who are said to be energetically present in her work. The female heart expressed through Flaubert's genius becomes a visceral experience through Ting Ling. *I Myself Am a Woman* is a lovely English translation of her collected writings.

Alice Walker (born 1944)

AMERICAN AUTHOR

Not everyone who grew up black on a Georgian tenant farm becomes a powerful political voice. And not every writer assumes the duty of broaching tough issues or advancing important causes. Alice Walker stepped forward on both fronts. Her deep connection with her roots has informed her profound personal evolution as well as her responsibility as a writer and as a symbol for African Americans and for women. She has tackled the toughest issues—the ravages of racism, the oppression of women, the abuse of children. Her poetry, short stories, and essays are as important as her Pulitzer Prize and American Book Award–winning *The Color Purple.* Composed, courageous, and convincing, Alice Walker's message is always clear. "The world, I believe, is easier to change than we think. And harder. Because the change begins with each one of us saying to ourselves, and meaning it: I will not harm anyone or anything . . . and there begins to be built a whole other community, a whole other family of people who are not related by color, blood, or sex— but by vision. That's how I feel, that I'm part of a whole community of great people, and it's not about race, it's about vision and what we think the world will be and should be."

Simone Weil (1909–1943)

FRENCH MYSTIC AND SOCIAL PHILOSOPHER

At the age of five Simone Weil refused to eat sugar because the French soldiers at the front during World War I had none. As a young woman she donated large portions of her small salary to exploited industrial workers. Highly educated, she worked in a factory with heavy machinery to learn firsthand the deadening effects of hard labor on the human spirit. And she died at thirty-four of self-imposed starvation as a declaration of alliance with French compatriots under German occupation. This amazing woman, reared in comfort and security, a gifted intellectual who was first in her class in philosophy and logic at the Sorbonne, never took a breath she did not wish to share with someone more in need of the oxygen. Her classmate Simone de Beauvoir said Weil was the envy of all for her supreme intelligence, but what Beauvoir admired most in her she observed at the moment when the news hit of a famine in China—Simone Weil wept. When told that the problem was not to make men happy but to find the reason for their existence, she retorted sharply, "It is easy to see you have never been hungry." A deep mystic and philosopher, Simone Weil, who was raised a Jew, interpreted Plato through the eyes of a reverent Christian; she dismantled Aristotle on behalf of the mystical tradition; she devoured Taoism and Hinduism and plumbed the depths of Eastern thought. Her most devout religion was her own moral conviction. Her posthumously published works were highly influential in French and English social thought. She is regarded as one of the principal thinkers of her century.

Eudora Welty (born 1909)

AMERICAN AUTHOR

The love of language one experiences in Eudora Welty's work is poetically expressed in her own description of how she felt about books from her earliest childhood. "It had been startling and disappointing to me to find out that story books had been written by *people*, that books were not natural wonders, coming up of themselves like grass . . . I cannot remember a time when I was not in love with them—with the books themselves, cover and binding and the paper they were printed on, with their smell and their weight and with their possession in my arms, captured and carried off to myself." From a small Mississippi town, Eudora Welty attended Mississippi State College for Women, earned a degree from the University of Wisconsin, and an MBA from Columbia. She returned to Mississippi to work for a local newspaper and radio station. With Katherine Anne Porter as her literary mentor, her fiction received increasing critical acclaim and her *The Optimist's Daughter* won the Pulitzer Prize. Her stories are grounded in her distinctly Southern roots, but her voice is a universal voice of humanness and hopefulness. The elegant simplicity with which she illustrates character and evokes feeling creates in her readers a sense that, wherever they grew up, this Mississippi girl was right next door. *The Golden Apples* and *The Collected Stories of Eudora Welty* are among her treasures.

Edith Wharton (1862–1937)

AMERICAN AUTHOR

At first glance, Edith Wharton was a comfortable woman who wrote stories about the privileged society to which she belonged. A deeper look at the characters in her Pulitzer Prize–winning novel, *The Age of Innocence,* reveals something more complex about its author. Beneath the starched collars and confining corsets of old New York's upper class rustles a "growing sense of unreality and insufficiency," an intensity of agonizing longing known only to impoverished beings. We also discover in Edith Wharton a marvelous writer. She plays language for the mellifluous sounds she surely heard in many a drawing room. *A Backward Glance,* her poetic autobiography, unveils the quality and fullness of nature that distinguishes great literary figures, those who from childhood withdrew from the worlds into which they were born to invent destinies in the world of books. "There was in me a secret retreat where I wished no one to intrude . . . words and cadences haunted it like songbirds in a magic wood . . . I wanted to steal away and listen when they called . . . my imagination lay there, coiled and sleeping, a mute hibernating creature, and at the least touch of common things—flowers, animals, words, especially the sound of words . . . book after book . . . I was never again, in my inmost self, wholly lonely or unhappy."

Marion Post Wolcott (1910–1990)

AMERICAN FINE-ART PHOTOGRAPHER

There is only one way to communicate the significance of Marion Post Wolcott—to hold up one of her photographs. Until one has seen her images in black and white, all the words in the world will be inadequate. Marion Post was among the brigade of Farm Security Administration documentary photographers who chronicled America as it pulled up its bootstraps and moved through the Depression. Her letters tell, with delightful color and candor, how this natural beauty lived by her wits on the back roads of America in the late thirties. At four and a half cents a mile on top of her meager wage, she drove alone through America's back country, washing her stockings in the basins of rickety motels, waiting around railway offices for Uncle Sam's shipments of film, and hitting the road again—another town, another slice of America, another portrait of a people. Marion Post elevated the task to the level of high art. She was a shooter. Some fifteen thousand photographs. Photographs that would one day hang in the Museum of Modern Art. Her letters reveal the extraordinary woman behind the lens of her camera.

Mary Wollstonecraft (1759–1797)

ENGLISH AUTHOR AND FEMINIST PIONEER

"The first object of laudable ambition is to obtain character as a human being, regardless of the distinction of sex." We can only begin to grasp the progressiveness of Mary Wollstonecraft's intellect when we realize that she made this declaration in 1790, a time when the only conceivable way for a woman to elevate herself in the world was through a prudent marriage. Almost two centuries have passed since she declared civil and educational equality to be the right of women. Identifying her as a feminist would be an inadequate comparison to a modern-day activist for women's rights; she was among the architects of the frame of thought from which concepts of equality arose. It has taken almost two hundred years for this remarkable woman to be recognized as the commanding intellect, literary luminary, and fearless reformist she was. Her personal life and suffering, which provided targets for her critics for these many years, reveal to the modern reader the totality of her humanity and her womanhood. So complete was Mary Wollstonecraft's humanness that I imagine a footnote of clarification to her *A Vindication of the Rights of Woman* referencing the passage: "Civilized women of the present century, with few exceptions, are only anxious to inspire love, when they ought to cherish a nobler ambition, and by their abilities and virtues exact respect." I believe she would have added that when one is allowed more than *one* aspiration or enterprise in life, there is no more noble ambition than to inspire love.

Machaelle Small Wright (born 1945)

AMERICAN NATURALIST

Some would find Machaelle Small Wright's *Behaving As If The God In All Life Mattered* as compelling as its title. It is not for everyone. She would either be ahead of her time or out of her tree, respectively. This is the amazing story of her life since childhood and of the launch of her "deva spirit"–inspired garden and nature center in Virginia which is called Perelandra ("of the heart," from the C. S. Lewis novel *Perelandra.*) To appreciate the ideas put forth in this unique little book, one would have to find the Findhorn Garden in Scotland an intriguing phenomenon; to be receptive to the idea that there are intelligences in nature that guard and protect and guide, spirits who are communicating, to those of us who will listen, that we must take care of our precious gifts of air and water and land; to understand that the consciousness with which we approach our natural resources and grow our food affects the quality of the nourishment we receive from the life around us; to believe that all of life is deeply interconnected and full of Divine energy which is entirely available to us if we are open to it. For some, Machaelle Small Wright's story will just not be their cup of carrot juice. I found it marvelous and memorable and way ahead of its time.

Marguerite Yourcenar (1903–1987)

BELGIAN-BORN FRENCH-AMERICAN AUTHOR

Even in the present exalted company, Marguerite Yourcenar stands out as the most erudite and remarkable of minds. Born in Brussels to a French father and Belgian mother, she was educated at home and began writing as a teenager. With the death of her father she became independently wealthy and traveled a great deal until she settled in America and taught comparative literature at Sarah Lawrence College. She continued to write only in French and challenged her writing abilities by changing her style with each new genre and work—poetry, plays, novels, reinterpretations of ancient Greek myths, translations of African spirituals and works by great English-language artists such as Virginia Woolf and Henry James. Her masterpiece, *Memoirs of Hadrien*, which brought both French and American acclaim, is a historical novel based on the fictionalized autobiographical letters of the second-century Roman Emperor. Her other historical novel, translated as *The Abyss*, is a biography of an imaginary sixteenth-century alchemist-physician. Marguerite Yourcenar distinguished herself through the sheer cerebral majesty with which she examined human destiny. She was the first woman to be elected to the Academie Francaise; and since the exclusive literary institution required French citizenship, the president of France granted her a special dual U.S.-French citizenship to facilitate her election. The interview *Open Eyes: Conversations with Matthiew Galey* is a wonderful glimpse at her raw genius.

Virginia Woolf (1882–1941)

BRITISH AUTHOR

In the case of Virginia Woolf, it would be inadequate to toil for a few well-chosen words to describe her as a woman, a gifted author, and a distinguished literary critic. It is also impossible to speak of her without interlacing her words throughout, for with icons of excellence and mastery, their own expression far surpasses any other descriptors for capturing their true essence. She said that all great literary figures are both inheritors and originators. What she herself gleaned and has given can be measured only by that faculty of soul that both inherits and originates, a silent somatic sense that finds its way into the world of words only through poetry. I will be forever in her debt for that magical moment of internal rearrangement provoked by communion with her spirit, the spirit poetically disguised as Shakespeare's sister's, which cries out to women who write. My life and my work have been enriched beyond imagining by the literature I have consumed as a result of that moment. Though *The Words of a Woman* contains the words of some fifty women, there are hundreds whose voices are as much a part of this work as their great works are alive in me. And for all of it—"the thousand women . . . who wrote as women write"—I am indebted to one moment with one book by one extraordinary woman. "Nature, in her most irrational mood, has traced in invisible ink on the walls of the mind a premonition which these great artists confirm; a sketch which only needs to be held to the fire of genius to become visible. When one so exposes it and sees it come to life one exclaims in rapture. But this is what I have always felt and known and desired!" Virginia Woolf's simple legacy—to all who write: "It is much more important to be oneself than anything else."

Jeanne de Vietinghoff (1875–1926)

BELGIAN-BORN FRENCH PHILOSOPHER

It was Marguerite Yourcenar who said that sometimes a book can lie neglected in a dark corner of a library for fifty or two thousand years until one day it is happened upon by a person who experiences it as though it were written just for them. This was my experience of Jeanne de Vietinghoff. I had actually searched for her books because of another reference by the supreme Yourcenar, whom she inspired as "the kind of soul who makes us believe the soul exists." Jeanne de Vietinghoff did not live an extraordinary life. She did not achieve anything more heroic than any devoted mother or true friend or fully formed loving human being. She wrote a few small books, meditations on life; only *The Understanding of Good* is in English translation. And in the very few libraries where her books can be found, they are cataloged as "philosophy." In the now-seven-year course of this project I have not encountered a single person, not a French scholar, literary authority, or philosophy professor, who had ever heard her name. Yet of all the hundreds of great works I consumed, it was with hers that I grasped the purpose of writing our deepest truths. For if one person in all of time is affected by our words as I was affected by Jeanne de Vietinghoff's, then our contribution to life has been immense. Her sincere heart spoke to the hearts of all who believe, without regard for definition or dogma, for formalization or delineation or demarcation. Her love and her faith knew no boundary; they filled the whole of her, and radiated from her like a life-giving force from the infinite source she served. I know of no other way to express my praise than to say that because I have known her I will never be the same.

ACKNOWLEDGMENTS

Grateful acknowledgment is extended to the authors and author representatives who granted permission to include excerpts from the following:

My Half Century by Anna Akhmatova, edited by Ronald Meyer, translated by Alexander Pushkin. Copyright © 1992 by Ardis Publishers. Reprinted by permission of Ardis Publishers.

Looking Back, Memoirs by Lou Andreas-Salome, edited by Ernest Pfeiffer, translated by Breon Mitchell.

The Life of the Mind by Hannah Arendt. Copyright © 1978 by Harcourt Brace & Company. Reprinted by permission of the publisher.

Freedom from Fear by Aung San Suu Kyi. Copyright © 1991 by Aung San Suu Kyi. Reprinted with the permission of the author.

Letters to her sister by Jane Austen.

Persuasion by Jane Austen.

All Said and Done, The Autobiography of Simone de Beauvoir by Simone de Beauvoir, translated by Patrick O'Brian.

An Hour with Charlotte Brontë, selections from Charlotte Brontë edited by Laura C. Halloway.

Five Essays Written in French by Emily Brontë.

Glimpses Into My Own Life and Literary Character by Elizabeth Barrett Browning.

On the Art of Fiction by Willa Cather.

Journey for Myself by Colette, translated by David LeVay. Copyright © 1971 by Peter Owen, Ltd. Reprinted with the permission of the publisher.

Memorandum by Madame Curie to the League of Nations Committee on Intellectual Cooperation, 1926.

Acknowledgments

Gift from the Sea by Anne Morrow Lindbergh. Copyright © 1955, 1975, and renewed 1983 by Anne Morrow Lindbergh. Reprinted by permission of Pantheon Books, a division of Random House, Inc.

The Journal of Katherine Mansfield by Katherine Mansfield, edited by J. Middleton Murry. Copyright © 1927 by Alfred A. Knopf, Inc. Copyright renewed 1955 by J. Middleton Murry. Reprinted by permission of Alfred A. Knopf, Inc., and the Society of Authors, on behalf of the Katherine Mansfield Estate.

West with the Night by Beryl Markham. Copyright © 1942, 1983 by Beryl Markham. Reprinted by permission of North Point Press, a division of Farrar Straus & Girox, Inc., Laurence Pollinger Limited, and the Estate of Beryl Markham.

Selected Poems by Gabriela Mistral, translated by Doris Dana. Copyright © 1971 by Doris Dana. Reprinted by arrangement with Doris Dana, c/o Joan Daves Agency as agent for the proprietor.

Mutant Message Down Under by Marlo Morgan. Copyright © 1991, 1994 by Marlo Morgan. Reprinted by permission of HarperCollins Publishers, Inc.

Cassandra by Florence Nightingale.

Letter "To 'A', 9 August 55" from *The Habit of Being, Letters of Flannery O'Connor,* selected and edited by Sally Fitzgerald. Copyright © 1979 by Regina Cline O'Connor. Reprinted by permission of Farrar, Straus & Giroux, Inc., and Harold Matson Company, Inc.

The Collected Essays and Occasional Writings of Katherine Anne Porter. Copyright © 1970 by Katherine Anne Porter. Published by Delacorte Press. Reprinted by permission of the Literary Estate of Katherine Anne Porter.

For the New Intellectual by Ayn Rand.

Lettres d'un voyageur by George Sand, translated by Sacha Rabinovitch and Patricia Thomson. Copyright © 1987 by Sacha Rabinovitch and Patricia Thomson. Reprinted by permission of Penguin Books, Ltd.

Sappho: A New Translation, poems and fragments by Sappho, translated by Mary Barnard. Copyright © 1958 by the Regents of the University of California; renewed 1984 by Mary Barnard. Reprinted by permission of the

ABOUT THE AUTHOR

CHRISTINE MARY MCGINLEY, originally from Walled Lake, Michigan, has been an advocate for the arts and humanities for more than twenty years, serving as executive director and fundraiser for cultural and educational institutions in Phoenix, Vail, Chicago, and Ann Arbor. She holds a degree in Consciousness and Communication which she designed herself through De Paul University's School for New Learning. She now lives in Mill Valley, California.

Anna Akhmatova ⋈ Lou Andreas-Salom

⋈ Jane Austen ⋈ Simone de Beauvoi

⋈ Elizabeth Barrett Browning ⋈ V

Bernadette Devlin McAliskey ⋈ En

(Hilda Doolittle) ⋈ Isadora Duncar

Margaret Fuller ⋈ Gildas (a spirit who

Alice James ⋈ Sarah Orne Jewett (⋈

⋈ Katherine Mansfield ⋈ Beryl Markh

Florence Nightingale ⋈ Flannery O'Co

George Sand ⋈ Sappho ⋈ May Sa

Gertrude Stein ⋈ Jing Ling ⋈ Jeanne

Eudora Welty ⋈ Edith Wharton ⋈

⋈ Virginia Woolf ⋈ Machaelle S